Praise for A Hidden Order

"This is like having a dolphin as your guide and mentor as you learn how to swim skillfully in the oceans of energies in which we all live. *A Hidden Order* is informative, inspiring, and practical. Truly the work of a master teacher."

—Al Siebert, Ph.D., author of *The Survivor Personality* and director of the Resiliency Center

"An intelligent and wonderful narrative about invisible pathways and crossroads that shape lives. Deep human interest, intriguing details, uplifting insights!"

—Ingo Swann

"*A Hidden Order* is a book of learning anew the ability to awaken the silent inner person waiting to be released."

—Ruth Berger, author of *They Don't See What I See* and *Medical Intuition*

"Winter Robinson not only has the courage to faithfully listen to her inner voice of wisdom, but she also takes actions that create the life she is meant to live. In *A Hidden Order* she shares her stories and the stories of others who are able to discover the blueprint of their lives. This book is inspiring and motivating for all who have the courage to follow the path of inner wisdom."

—Carole Lynne, author of *How To Get a Good Reading from a Psychic Medium* and *Heart and Sound*

"With elegant simplicity and autobiographical integrity, Winter Robinson offers the reader the keys to understanding her life's unique purpose. This book is an invitation to live life not as an observer but as a full participant. An invitation we dare not refuse."

—Paula M. Reeves, Ph.D., author of *Women's Intuition* and *Heart Sense*

Also by Winter Robinson

Intuitions: Seeing with the Heart

Remembering: A Gentle Reminder of Who You Are

A Hidden Order

Uncover Your Life's Design

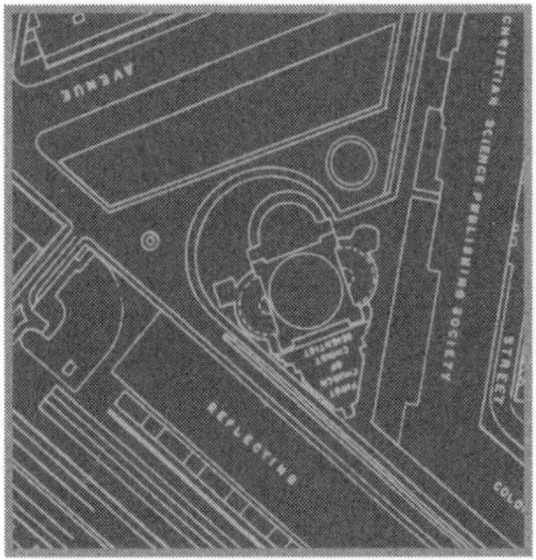

Winter Robinson

Red Wheel
Boston, MA / York Beach, ME

First published in 2004 by Red Wheel/Weiser, LLC
York Beach, ME
With offices at: 368 Congress Street Boston, MA 02210
www.redwheelweiser.com

Library of Congress Cataloging-in-Publication Data
Robinson, Winter.
A hidden order : uncover your life's design / Winter Robinson.
p. cm.
Includes bibliographical references.
ISBN 1-59003-084-2
1. Self-actualization (Psychology)—Miscellanea.
2. Parapsychology. I. Title.
BF1045.S44R63 2004
158.1—dc22

2004013891

Typeset in Minion by Joyce C. Weston Design
Printed in Canada
TCP
11 10 09 08 07 06 05 04 8 7 6 5 4 3 2 1

For Michael

Contents

Acknowledgments

First and foremost, I thank my parents for agreeing to be my guides in this life. From the very beginning, their openness to the magic of the Universe—to those things we cannot see and do not understand—set the stage for my life. Although they are no longer in physical form, their voices speak to me every day.

I am eternally indebted to the hundreds of individuals who were willing to share their remarkable stories with me. Even though not all of them made it into print, each narrative played an important role in helping me know that there *is* a blueprint—a hidden order to our Universe.

I cannot fully express my love and thanks to my good friend and writing mentor Jennifer Monn. Jenn has the ability to always understand what I am attempting to convey and, with unselfish guidance, bring clarity to my projects—reminding me to "keep it simple." I am truly grateful that she is in my life.

For her generous assistance in *all* matters of my life, I thank Ellen Foss, my gracious friend and capable assistant who showed up just when I needed her. Not only did she turn my requests for information about teas, rituals, and invocations into form—she fed the cats, watered the geese, answered numerous queries from individuals, and even set up my spinning bike so that all I had to do was leave the computer to work out.

I thank the entire team at Red Wheel/Weiser, especially Robyn Heisey-Rowe, my publisher and editor who immediately understood what this book was all about and who wholeheartedly supported this project from the beginning. And I thank Jill Rogers for holding my hand, answering my numerous questions, and patiently reading my handwritten edits.

I thank also Yudika Seko for helping me get *A Hidden Order* into a file format that was readable by Red Wheel; and for the loving care

Yudi, Brent Atkinson, and Christine Bragg took of our home and animals while we were on the road.

I especially thank Marilyn DiBonaventuro for believing that the story of the *Harkness* should be told again, and Vance and Sari Bunker for their willingness to tell it.

Thanks go to Jennifer Vanderwerf for believing in magic and believing in me and special thanks go to my friends at Hartford Family Institute for being my office away from home. I could not have manifested a more holistic group of practitioners to work among.

It goes without saying that I could not have written this book without the support and guidance of Barbara Bowen, my agent—editor extraordinaire and trusted friend. Her patient questioning and editing of my manuscript helped me get my many differentiated thoughts in a "straight line." Thank you, Barb, from the bottom of my heart.

I thank my wonderful support system of friends who have tributed their help along the way. You know who you are, and I deeply thank you. I also want to thank Margaret Naeser for introducing me to Chinese medicine and continually keeping me informed about complementary medicine; my good friend Linda Edwards for guiding me on this journey by introducing me to the I Ching and taking me to see my first psychicJean Strickland for generously sharing her reference books, tapes, thoughts, and—especially—her talents; and Joy Hampp for sharing her original ideas and insights about a hidden order every month for the past two years as this book unfolded. I also thank Marie Southwick for her wise counsel and loan of what seemed to be every book and paper ever written about synchronicity, and Barbara Myers for being my personal deep-ecology activist, teacher, and boddhisattva.

Most of all, I want to thank my husband, Michael, the center o life, lover, partner, co-creator, and co-explorer. He is my toughest editor and strongest supporter. For many hours he questioned and debated the merits of this topic, leading me to clarify my beliefs. He always brings out the best in me and never settles for anything less. I am so fortunate to have found my "Noble Friend" who sees what I cannot see.

Introduction

It is my belief that truth arises in the present moment, is evident in its simplicity, and must be experienced to be understood. We don't need great or beautiful books to recognize truth. Books have a way of passing information around, allowing us to distance ourselves from their subject matter, indeed from life itself. Because we can read about it, we think that we don't have to do anything.

A Hidden Order is not meant to be a book that you read quickly, or once, and put aside. It is a manual, carefully designed to help you discover and direct your life into a future that you take part in creating. I encourage you to actively participate in the suggested exercises, invocations, and rituals included at the end of each chapter.

When our inner (internal, spiritual) and outer (physical) worlds meet, a hidden order reveals itself. At least, that's what I believe. The purpose of this book is to assist you in bringing these worlds together.

A Hidden Order is divided into two parts: A Gentle Tap and Master Practices. In part 1, A Gentle Tap, you will read true stories of love and relationships, life and death, dreams, intuitions, and guidance that will illustrate the invisible blueprint, the hidden order, at work in all our lives. Each chapter contains practical experiential exercises, including daybook or journal writing, rituals, invocations, and some words of wisdom, which I call Food for Thought.

Often we simply read a book and never act on what we read. It is easier to just pick up another book and keep reading rather than actually *do* the practice, whatever it may be. When we acquire information indirectly from books, we may intellectually know what we read, but we don't necessarily take the principles to heart and put them into practice.

The goal of the experiential practice sections is simple—to make it easy for you to be proactive in creating (and following) a conscious, participatory, spiritual practice to discover your blueprint—the hidden order underlying your life. I have made the concepts practical, making sure important details are included.

There are various items that you will need to help you with the individual rituals and exercises. These items are mentioned at the beginning of each activity. Before you run out to the nearest ritual supply mart, remember that ritual has been around much longer than our shopping malls. Rituals are nature-based. We use items from nature because they are in touch with the flow of the Universe, of a hidden order. If you don't want to use pennies to consult the *I Ching,* then I suggest that you grow your own yarrow, or visit a local herb farm that may have yarrow stalks lying around. Beads can also be used to generate randomness.

As for many of the books mentioned, scour the used-book stores. Check with friends who are giving away books they no longer use. See how creative you can be to obtain what you need. But in case you find yourself in a pinch, I have included an appendix to help you find sources where some more hard-to-find items, such as Chinese herbs, may be purchased.

In part 2, Master Practices, four master exercises form the necessary foundation for exploring the ideas presented in *A Hidden Order.* These practices are meant to be part of your daily routine. Although I put Ego and Beliefs first, and Following the Breath—Quieting the Mind second, in reality they go hand in hand. It would be impossible to follow your breath and quiet your mind without having your ego pop in and question your belief about *why* you are following your breath. Like all things, there is no one "right" order to do your master exercises.

One or more of the Master Practices are referred to at the end of each chapter in part 1. But even though a chapter may only mention one Master Practice, as you search for your life's design you might find that all four practices keep showing up. You will constantly question your beliefs, asking yourself, "Is this (belief) true? Why do I think so?" Following your breath will become second nature, and you will wonder how you ever managed to not set your intention for what you wished to create, or how you could have ignored your dreams for so many years.

After reading each chapter, turn to part 2 and follow the suggested Master Practice. Then return to the experiential section of the chapter. This section will prompt you to journal in your daybook, practice a simple mindfulness exercise for the day, and ponder a challenging Food for Thought. The experiential sections close with self-explanatory invocations and rituals.[1]

I believe that a hidden order is rapidly making itself known, suggesting to every one of us that there is a spiritual evolution going on; that we have the potential to rid the world of fear, confusion, chaos, and greed and bring humankind into harmony with nature and the cosmos. If we foster our own spiritual growth, we advance the well-being of the whole world. It's our choice.

Part 1

A Gentle Tap

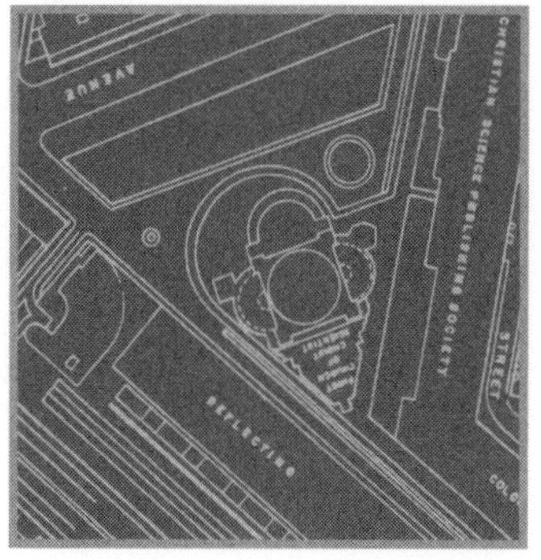

1
My Journey

The world is not to be put in order, the world is order incarnate. It is for us to put ourselves in unison with this order.

—Henry Miller

In the summer of 1981, after ending my career directing programs in mental health for a local university, I took a position with the Office of the Attorney General for the Commonwealth of Virginia. Two years later, my structured world of law and mental health turned inside out. While working as a legal analyst I had a precognitive experience that was so detailed and accurate it changed the way I saw reality.

One morning my boss requested a list of several documents we would need for an upcoming trial. Without giving it a second thought, I quickly wrote down the titles and document numbers, handed the list to my secretary, and returned to work. She came to my desk shortly afterward and said, "These are not what Karen asked for. These are random letters that I recently boxed up. They are going to the state archives this afternoon." I could not believe my ears. Confused by my mistake, I wrote down the correct titles and document numbers and went to lunch.

When I returned, my secretary met me at the door. Totally out of the blue, a new lawsuit had been filed against the commonwealth. It turned out that the initial titles and document numbers I had written down were the very ones needed for our defense in this new case. I had somehow gone to the future and retrieved information we would need for a case we did not know we had. Thanks to this insight, the box was not sent to the archives and the documents were easily pulled.

This single event, like a gentle tap, rekindled a side of myself that I had allowed to fade: my fascination with the invisible side of life. As a child I was an avid reader. I would spend hours curled up in my favorite wingback chair reading ghost stories, Edgar Cayce books, UFO accounts—anything that suggested there was an unseen element to our reality.

I was fascinated by my grandmother who knew things beyond the familiar realm of the senses. She lived on a cotton farm in the middle of Georgia, without a telephone. We lived in the mountains of North Carolina, a good ten hours away. Our visits were always random and spontaneous. She never had any advance warning that we were on the way and she would always be ready: fresh sheets on the bed, dinner prepared. And she would be waiting for us on the front porch.

"But how does she know?" I would ask my mother. "How did she know what time we'd arrive when we didn't tell her we were coming?"

"She just knows."

During each visit, I would sit on my grandma's knee, mesmerized, as she told stories of the unseen—stories about ghosts and spirits, fairies and magic—stories that ultimately primed me for a mystical experience and led me to search for Truth.

That was how all this began. But that fateful day in the attorney general's office left me with an inexplicable feeling that I was being pushed toward a different future than the one I had planned. I became obsessed with discovering how precognition worked. I tried to figure out the meaning of life. I started scrolling backward in my mind, looking at all of my life experiences—the good, the sorrowful, the ecstatic, and those I would rather forget. I laid the time and place of my birth, my parents, friends, and relatives, my talents, education, and meaningful coincidences side-by-side. I saw something that I had not noticed before. I saw an unseen design—an order to the way my life was unfolding. Separate, random events began to fall into some kind of pattern when I looked at the whole picture.

I had been a surprise to my parents who, after seventeen years of childless marriage expected to remain that way. Once I arrived on this Earth, I had several close calls with death. When I was four years old, wielding a copper rod that was my magic wand, I stuck it into a live fuse box; at age nine, while swimming on my own, I tried a difficult dive and knocked myself out on the bottom of our swimming pool. Several years later, alone again, I fell through the ice in that same pool.

But probably the most memorable of these close calls came when I was a young adult. I was booked on Piedmont Airlines to fly to Philadelphia because my airline of choice, United, was fully booked. After checking in, even though United was sold out, I left my name on their waiting list. The planes left within five minutes of each other, so it shouldn't have really mattered which airline I flew. But as I sat in the terminal, I became more convinced that I did not want to fly on the Piedmont plane. I kept checking with the United ticket agent, and just as Piedmont issued their last call to board, the United attendant called my name. They had a vacant seat and I took it. Ten minutes into the Piedmont flight, the airplane collided with a Cessna. There were no survivors.

Shortly after my earth-shaking precognitive experience, Linda, a colleague of mine, "accidentally" picked up her copy of the Chinese Oracle, the *I Ching*, along with her casework files, and brought it to the office. "I think this is for you," she said, waving it in front of my face. "Are you familiar with the *I Ching*?" I had to admit that I had never heard of it.

Linda told me that in China the *I Ching*, known in English as *The Book of Changes*,[1] is considered to be the oldest continuously used book in human history, a great classic, and the foundation of Chinese scholarship. Its origin traces back almost 5,000 years to a time when the venerable sage Fu-hsi noticed signs of impending events, observed patterns in nature, and organized the signs into a system that anyone could use.

"Think of a question that you want the answer to," she said. "It's important that you place yourself in the center of the question, in the middle of this point in time. Then the past and future can express themselves in the present moment."

After asking me to pull out three pennies, she showed me how to toss the pennies and read the corresponding hexagram they formed. "Take it seriously," she said. "Because it reveals how your entire destiny is unfolding."

After she left, I closed my office door. Curious, excited, and probably more than a little apprehensive, I asked myself, "What *do* I want to know?"

I wanted to know what was going on in my life. Since my prescient experience, reality had taken on an added dimension.

I threw the coins and carefully wrote down the lines as they appeared. My first *I Ching* hexagram was Hexagram 1—Creative Power with no changing lines. The ancient Chinese realized that the Universe is constantly changing: day to night, winter to spring, life to death. Moving lines show the flow of this change. Thus, a hexagram without changing lines was a deeply significant omen. I felt that Linda was right, my destiny *was* making itself known.

> The force of this time is the primal directive that propels us into our destinies, regardless of what our reasoning or recalcitrant minds may think. What you create now will be the basis and inspiration for what you experience next. As a result of any action you now take, your fate will be sealed. You may always trace back to the beginning, but there will never be an end to what you are about to set in motion.[2]

I cannot tell you exactly how I felt when I read these words, except that they resonated within the depth of my being. I was connecting with something that I knew to be true. It might have looked like chance, but it was definitely more than chance. Still, the experimental psychologist part of me had to toss the coins again to test the probability that the coins would fall in the same position a second time. They did. That morning in the attorney general's office was the only time, in now twenty years of tossing the *I Ching*, that the coins have fallen to the Hexagram 1 with *no* changing lines.

The *I Ching* reinforced a thought that had been churning in the back of my mind: *there are no accidents*. Either everything in the Universe had to be an accident, a coincidence, or nothing was. It could not be chance that I was working for the attorney general in the first place, that my colleague, Linda, had accidentally picked up her *I Ching Workbook* that morning, or that I received *this* message at exactly *this* point in time.[3]

Two years earlier I had decided that I wanted to leave my faculty position at a local university and become the director of training for the state's Department of Mental Health. When the position opened up, I actively pursued it. At the time I was under a state contract to coordinate all of the department's mental health training and education. I was well liked and had support from the highest levels. There was no doubt I was qualified to do the job. I thought that I got along well with the director of human resources, the woman who, if I got the position, would be my boss. After all, she had repeatedly told me that she wanted me in the position. I trusted her.

The first and second rounds of interviews came and went. No one was hired and the position was re-advertised. I was interviewed again. No decision was made. Six months, then a year passed. The Department of Mental Health brought in an out-of-state team of management professionals to interview candidates. My inside sources told me that I emerged as the number one candidate and that most certainly I would be hired within the next week. Weeks, then months passed with no decision. At last the announcement came that a virtually unknown Ms. X had been given the job.

Although I was floored by the decision, it did not keep me from stumbling into my destiny. I resigned from the position I occupied, without a clue as to what I would do next. Within hours of handing in my resignation, an assistant attorney general in the Office of the Attorney General called. I had been mentioned as being someone capable of helping them build the defense in a First Amendment case against the Department of Mental Health.

What started as a three-week interim position became a fascinating three-year career and turned out to be a major turning point in my life. The interesting twist of fate was that I had to build the defense for the actions taken against the plaintiffs by the director of human resources—the woman who had not given me the director of training position.

Now the Oracle's words that said a primary directive was propelling me into my destiny rang true. Driven by my need to know more, one of my next steps was to visit a psychic in Virginia Beach. Perhaps this visit did seal my fate. The psychic predicted that I would marry my true soulmate within three years. At that time, I was married. In fact, I had been married to the same man for fifteen years and had no conscious intention of divorcing him.

Nonetheless, within the space of a year, I left the marriage and moved to Rhode Island. Several months after I moved, I had a lucid dream of being with a familiar stranger who kissed me. Although in my dream I was angry that he was so presumptuous, the next morning I wrote in my dream journal that I liked his kiss. A few months later I woke in the middle of the night to a clear voice that said, "Waiting for Michael."

Before we met, Michael went to a psychic in Maine. He had been a bachelor for ten years but the psychic told him, "Your life is going to really change. You're going to get married. She's brunette, five feet seven inches tall. . . ." He apparently had immediately thrown up his hands and said, "Stop! Don't tell me anymore."

Seven months after Michael had stopped the psychic, I was heading out of the house to teach a weekend seminar in Chicago. I had just called a taxi to take me to the airport when the telephone rang. It was the training director for the Monroe Institute who wanted me to fly to Virginia that same weekend and lead their next program. Although I had never canceled a scheduled seminar before, I felt that I had to accept the director's request to train this particular program in Virginia. I canceled my Chicago appearance and flew to Charlottesville.

As it turned out, Michael was a participant in that program. For some mysterious reason, we said only seventeen words to each other the entire week. Our brief exchange took place one evening when I was late for dinner and took the only seat available, which was next to him.

"Do you know how intimidated I am that you can read my mind?" he asked. (He had heard of my reputation for being very psychic and able to read people's minds.)

"Yes. Why is that?"

At that moment my co-trainer pulled me away from the table. Michael and I did not finish the conversation. Nine months later, when our destined paths crossed again, I learned that my response to his question had set in motion his own search for understanding. He began to look deeply to find out why he was uncomfortable that someone else could read his mind.

Extraordinary synchronicities continue to help define who I am today. For example, I was asked to take part in the research component that investigated human consciousness at the Monroe Institute. One of the projects was to explore the concept of remote viewing, a fancy name for psychic visioning. During one of my sessions the cartoon character, Yosemite Sam, appeared in my mind. At the time, I called Yosemite Sam "Sam the Pirate." (Michael later gave me his proper name.) I had never been a fan of cartoons, even as a child, and I did not know who he was. So the fact that a cartoon character showed up in what I thought was a "very serious" experiment got my attention.

I had been well trained by the staff not to edit my information, not to eliminate anything that appeared to go against my academic knowledge, experience, or belief systems. I was to describe in detail *everything* that I saw, heard, or felt. So I did, and I was able to accurately diagnose certain medical conditions of the person who was monitoring my session. Not having an interest in medicine or a medical background, I wondered, "Why me? Doctors and medical students should be the ones having this kind of insight."

The following summer I learned the answer to my question, "Why me?" I attended a conference in Virginia. I had arrived late to a session and there was only one empty seat in the entire auditorium. I sat down and then during the break I introduced myself to the stranger next to me. For some reason, I told him about Yosemite Sam and that I seemed to be able to diagnose people at a distance. He smiled and told me that he was Chris Hedsel,[4] a faculty member from Brown University's medical school. He had always been interested in Edgar Cayce and was curious to find out how much useful medical information could be obtained intuitively. Our work together began three months later when he phoned and asked, "What can you tell me about one of my medical students who has just been diagnosed with Hodgkins disease?" I told him what I saw. Chris and I worked in this manner, by telephone, for a year. He would call with the name of a person and I would tell him what I sensed. It was not long before I discovered that I was also answering questions for another faculty member in the medical school, one who had scientific theories concerning what happens to the flow of blood during trauma.

From my experience working with the faculty from the medical school, I began to feel more and more strongly that the ability to diagnose intuitively should be part of the curriculum for medical students, nurses, and other health practitioners. Chris and I discussed this at length, and eventually proposed this type of training to other interested faculty members at Brown. When I moved to Rhode Island, I began to teach intuitive diagnosis, "the art of medicine," as the Dean of Students put it, to a group of medical students, physicians, and social workers.

As I continued to look back over the journey of my life, I began to see a previously unseen pattern emerge from the various events. I realized I had enough stories to fill a book. And that's what I set out to do. But when I began to share my thoughts about the project, I discovered that everyone has stories that show the magic and wonder of a hidden order. I began to receive hundreds of letters, calls, and emails from people who had their own amazing stories to tell. I decided to expand the project and include their miraculous stories because they demonstrate that a hidden order shows itself to everyone.

My introduction to the *I Ching* started me on a life-long search for tools, ideas, and methods that would allow me to learn as much as I could about the way things move through the Universe—about what I am calling a hidden order. I hope that by sharing both these stories and tools you will also discover the patterns in your life and come to a greater understanding of the cosmos and yourself, and of the sameness between the two.

Experiential Practice

The following exercises are designed to help you get started on your search for your life's design and to introduce tools that you will be working with throughout the book.

Beginning with the Master Practice, Following the Breath—Quieting the Mind, and the Tool Bag's suggestion of being fully aware in the moment, you are given a foundation to discover all that is important in the present moment. When you are fully present, a hidden order shows itself.

The review of your life and looking for the common thread; asking for help; and learning to consult the *I Ching*, frequently referenced throughout this book, are concepts and tools you will return to again and again.

Getting Started

Read and perform the Master Practice exercise, Following the Breath—Quieting the Mind, in chapter 10, then continue with the exercises below.

Daybook

One of my favorite ways of connecting with a hidden order, as well as of gaining intuitive insight, is to write in a daybook or journal. My journal includes synchronistic events, my moods, quotes, intuitive hunches, assessment of when things went the way I thought they would and when they didn't, and dreams and thoughts that I remember when I wake in the night. I encourage you to keep your own daybook to help you cultivate your intuitive senses and to uncover some of the hidden patterns in your own life.

There are a few things to keep in mind when you use your daybook. First, keep your daybook handy. You will use it not only for the exercises in this book, but for meaningful coincidences and your intuitive hunches—your gut feelings that you will want to record whenever they occur. Allow your ideas to flow. Keep your pen or pencil on the paper while you write. No editing. Don't stop to decide whether you think something is accurate, or worth including. If it occurs to you, write it down. Sometimes you won't know if a hunch or idea is accurate or valid until long after you've written it down. As you start to observe synchronistic events you may think, "This is just my imagination." That's fine. Write them down anyway. (Remember: I learned that my imagination *was* real.)

Once you begin to work with the exercises in this book, you will start to see the meaningful coincidences, or synchronicities, in your life, and they will occur more and more often. It has been my experience that when I act as if this invisible force is with me, all sorts of unusual incidents, meetings, and material assistance come my way. They are part of a hidden order making itself known.

Begin your daybook journaling by looking for the blueprint that flows through your life. Look back over your life, starting with the present moment. Survey all of your life experiences—good, bad, fortuitous, unhappy—from the perspective that there is an invisible force, a blueprint, that connects all of them together. All of these events are related and have brought you to this point in time.

Review these milestones, looking for a central theme. You may also have several sub-themes. Now answer the following questions in your journal.

- What events were major turning points in your life?
- What unexpected opportunities have appeared?
- When did you seemingly have "divine intervention"?
- What mystical experiences have you had?
- What theme is occurring and/or recurring in your life right now? How does it tie in with your life up to this point?
- Is there a theme that seems to point you in a certain direction?

Tool Bag

Put your "to do" list aside for today. Practice being fully in the moment. The only tool you need is the awareness of your breath in the present moment.

Stop, sit down, and intentionally notice your breathing several times throughout the day. This can be for ten minutes, or ten seconds. Fully accept how you feel and what you think is happening. Don't try to change anything. Simply breathe and let things be. When you're ready, hold this feeling of acceptance as you continue with your day, and if you like, you can pick up your "to do" list.

Food for Thought

> All that is visible must grow beyond itself, extend into the realm of the invisible. Thereby it receives true consecration and clarity and takes firm root in the cosmic order.
>
> *I Ching* (Hexagram 50)
> —Richard Wilhelm

Invocation

Invocations are used to ask for help in a heartfelt, thoughtful way. Throughout this book I suggest that you become accustomed to asking for help in order to connect with a hidden order. Asking for help does not necessarily mean it has to come from "outside." Help can come from a more expanded part of yourself, what some call a "higher self." Or from whatever you consider Source, the Universe, guardians, angels. The key is that you are consciously asking to expand your awareness beyond a limited viewpoint. You are asking for assistance in pulling your focus back so you can see the *big* picture. This is different from asking God, or a Source that you perceive to be greater than you to do it for you.

Stand barefoot, with your feet slightly apart and your arms hanging loosely at your sides but not touching your body. Take a deep breath, and as you inhale, say to yourself: "I ask for the highest Source of information to be present. Help me expand my awareness and see more clearly." Pause, then without closing your throat, ask for strength, protection, and guidance. Exhale.

Do this two more times.

Always say your invocations three times. The repetition focuses our intention and heightens our consciousness.

What are you invoking? When you do this exercise, you will be invoking strength or your personal power, which will protect you from anything you fear, even from fear itself. In particular it will protect you from your own chattering mind. You are also invoking guidance, help to find out where to go, which path to take, and what choice to make. You may want to ask to become more acutely aware of the guidance of your hidden order as it makes itself known.

If you have a specific request, or a question you are seeking an answer to, ask it at the end of the third invocation. Close by saying something that feels like a natural ending to you. It may be a simple, "Thank You," "Blessings," "Blessed Be," "Amen," "So May It Be," or some other form of gratitude and closure.

Ritual

Each of the chapters in this book contains a ritual. Rituals are not to be confused with ceremonies, which are acts of confirmation. Many religious rites are actually ceremonies, not rituals. We use ritual to create a sacred space in which to focus our intent, be it for divining information, healing, manifesting, seeking a state of grace, or giving thanks. Because many rituals have been repeated throughout history, we draw upon the energy and collective consciousness of all who have performed the ritual previously.

Consulting the I Ching

This ritual uses the ancient art of the *I Ching*. The *I Ching* has been used for centuries to isolate the present moment and predict the future. By dropping three coins on a flat surface six times, or by dividing and counting yarrow stalks, you briefly stop time. The idea is similar to hitting "pause" on a DVD player in order to examine the scene in detail. The *I Ching* asks you to phrase your question carefully as you toss the coins or select the yarrow stalks. In this manner you align your self and your circumstances with the Universe's unfolding blueprint. When you receive the answer, treat it respectfully, ponder its significance, and act according to its guidance. By doing so, you gain insight into your own destiny. The more you use the *I Ching*, the more you will discover that this intricate and perplexing world is something that you have intimately understood all along.

You will want to have your personal copy of the *I Ching* available. Although there are many different versions, my preference is R. L. Wing's, *The I Ching Workbook.*[5] The directions are simple to follow and the hexagrams easy to interpret. (The Bollingen Series of *I Ching,*[6] translated by Richard Wilhelm, is another edition favored by many. For me, it is a little harder to understand.)

Find a quiet, orderly room. Bathe and dress in comfortable clothes. Take your telephone off the hook. If you like, burn incense. Make certain that you are alone and will not be disturbed.

Focus on why you are consulting the *I Ching.* Spend some time thinking about your question. Describe your problem or symptom. Write it down as clearly as you can.

Following the basic instructions in your *I Ching* book, toss the coins or divide your yarrow sticks to create a hexagram made up of six lines which, when read from bottom to top, represent images of everything that happens in heaven and on Earth. They are always in a state of change, flowing from one occurrence to another, just as our physical world is always changing.

In *Watching the Tree,*[7] Adeline Yen Mah recommends dividing yarrow sticks rather than tossing coins, "because the ritual of dividing sticks solemnizes the occasion. It also takes longer. Coin-tossing takes about two minutes, whereas dividing sticks may take from twenty to sixty minutes."

Once you arrive at the hexagram, take time to reflect on the answer. This is your time to experience a hidden order speaking directly to you.

2
Basic Principles: Creative Order

> Everything is determined, the beginning as well as the end, by forces over which we have no control. It is determined for the insect, as well as for the star. Human beings, vegetables, or cosmic dust, we all dance to a mysterious tune, intoned in the distance by an invisible piper.
>
> —Albert Einstein

There is an order to our natural world that we often take for granted. We need the photosynthesis of plants for the air we breathe. Plants, in turn, depend on the carbon dioxide produced by us and the nitrogen made by the bacteria at their roots. Together we create and maintain the conditions necessary for life. Quantum physicist David Bohm calls this the *explicate order*—the physical world as we know it in day-to-day reality.

But when we see the explicate order, what, in fact, we are seeing is only the surface of a hidden *implicate order*—the underlying, inexplicable force that seems almost mystical as it displays unseen connections. I believe the implicate order can present itself in many ways: a telephone call from an old friend just as you thought of them; a message from a departed loved one that comes to you in a dream; or meeting someone for the first time and feeling as if you have known them forever.

After working as an intuitive for twenty years, over thousands of sessions, helping people find answers to questions about their health, career, romantic relationships, and ultimately, questions about the nature of life, like "Why am I here?" or "What is my purpose?" I have come to believe that our lack of understanding of this basic order is the source of the disharmony in our lives—spiritually, personally, economically, globally, universally. We often feel victim to circumstances, to some "other" group or person, because we don't understand that we are connected to something much greater than our little selves.

In the work I have done during the past two decades, I've encountered certain recurring themes. They just kept showing up over and over again in the books I read, the experiences I had, in seminars I taught, and in my individual work with students. From these themes I developed nine guiding principles that have helped me understand reality and my relationship to it. I know there is a plan—a deeper meaning to life even if we cannot see it. I offer these principles to you as a guide. May they do for you what they continue to do for me.

The Nine Guiding Principles

1. An invisible hidden order underlies all existence.

Ancient teachings are a rich source of information about the natural order of life.

In 571 BC Lao Tzu, founder of Taoism, wrote of the hidden divine influence and called it the *tao*—the way of nature. The *tao* is powerful, invisible, inaudible, hidden, and nameless. Change is the only constant in the *tao.* And for every action there is a reaction, so the cosmos always remains balanced.

The Kabbalah, said to have originated during the Middle Ages when the rabbis studied ancient cryptic texts, also says that our world is ordered. The Kabbalah describes our world as a reflection of, and in symbiotic relationship with, other realms of reality. No event is commonplace, and every experience has a mystical meaning and is significant.

This concept of an ordered Universe in which we live more than one lifetime appears in early Christian doctrines, beginning with the texts of the Hermetic Gnostics, thought to be the original followers of Jesus. The Gnostics held that nothing happens by chance—everything is connected.

Of all the ancient texts,doctrines, and myths, it is the legend of the Holy Grail that triggers some alchemical process in my cellular memory. The legend, considered by some to be one of the most complex, cryptic mystical doctrines in existence,[1] holds a special place in my heart. When I need affirmation that a hidden order is at work, all I have to do is remember how the legend entered my life.

Michael Arthur Robinson and I had plans to be married in Maine. And we had hoped to travel to Peru prior to our wedding. In spite of the fact that our travel agent knew about our plans for six months, she never booked our tickets. After several frustrating calls to her, she was dismissed and Michael took over. Three days later he had managed to book two seats, albeit at inconvenient travel times, that would get us to Lima. My role in planning the trip was to gather as much information as possible about the Andes, Machu Picchu, and the Amazon Basin. I started with the state department's travel advisory:

> Care should be exercised at all times. There have been several recent bombings and explosions. The US and UK governments have issued alerts on the potential for further terrorism. We recommend that you do not travel to Peru unless absolutely necessary.

That same week an article appeared in our local paper about a man who conducted tours to Peru. "What a break," Michael said. "I'll give him a call."

I heard half of the conversation. "Speak Spanish . . . no . . . Shining Path guerrillas . . . you wouldn't?" Long pause. "No, I've never been to Glastonbury."

Michael hung up and confirmed what I had suspected. "He said don't go, especially if you don't speak Spanish. On his last trip he was nose-to-nose with a machine gun held by the rebels. Because he spoke Spanish he talked his way out of it. Out of the blue, he asked me if we had ever been to Glastonbury, England."

He had barely gotten "England" out of his mouth when an old friend from Washington, DC called. "I just returned from Glastonbury, England," she said. "Have you ever been there?"

Two weeks later we were in Glastonbury, England. Our flights, lodging, and car rental had fallen smoothly into place. Glastonbury felt very familiar, almost like home. We looked at each other and said, "Let's get married here!"

Easier said than done. It was Easter—lots of people get married at Easter. We were both divorced. In England if you are divorced you cannot be married in a church, the registrar has to do it. *If* the registrar could fit us in, the authorities in London had to see our divorce papers and approve of our union. And last, but not least, we had to establish a fifteen-day residence in England.

The obstacles seemed insurmountable. A chilly spring rain started to fall and tears of disappointment rolled down my cheeks. Michael suggested we drop by the Chalice Well, known for its healing waters. According to some traditions, the Grail vessel, a mysterious object said to hold the blood of the crucified Christ, was hidden in this spring.

"What are you—two ducks out in this downpour?" the woman asked, "And why are you looking so unhappy?" Willa, the warden of the well was speaking. Merlin the Magician flashed through my mind when I turned to see who had spoken. She wore a long dark cape and her eyes sparkled behind the hood that hung loosely over her head. Physically she was shorter than my five feet seven inches, but her distinct energy made me think she was at least six feet tall.

I explained the situation to her.

"Tsk, tsk. Just use my home as your residence." She picked up a pen, wrote her address on a piece of paper and handed it to me. "Give this to the registrar. He knows me." Thanking her for her kindness I stuffed the paper into my pocket. There seemed to be too many difficulties to overcome.

The next morning there was only one other guest in the breakfast room at our bed and breakfast. The large, burly, dark-haired man asked what we were doing in Glastonbury.

"We're just trying to get married," Michael said. This was very unlike Michael, who was not prone to divulging personal information to strangers.

"Until you are committed, nothing will happen . . . you will always be ineffective at what you are trying to do," the man said. "The moment you commit to each other, Providence will move for you. All of the things that you think are impossible will occur. As a result of your decision, a whole stream of events will bring favorable, unforeseen incidents, meetings, and material assistance that you never could have dreamed of your way. There is power and magic in committing." He lifted his coffee mug in a toast. "I suggest you commit . . . now." Michael and I looked at each other and smiled. We skipped breakfast and headed for the registrar's office.

The registrar asked for our address. I pulled the paper out of my pocket. It read, "Little St. Michael's Chalice Well." In that moment my doubts evaporated and I knew we would be married in England.

While the powers in London reviewed our divorce papers, and we waited the time necessary for residency, Michael and I headed north to Scotland. As long as I had known him, Michael had been fascinated with medieval arms and armor. A sword would make a nice wedding present for Michael, I reasoned. However, as we traveled, I looked high and low—all over England, Scotland, Wales, and Ireland—and could not find the sword that felt "right." His present would have to wait, perhaps indefinitely.

We set the spring equinox as the time and the Chalice Well as the location of our ceremony. Our wedding day dawned warm and sunny, but minutes before our ritual was to begin, dark clouds loomed and rain threatened. As I struggled with the thought of being married in the rain, Willa appeared, just as I suspect Merlin would have done centuries earlier.

"There is a room inside where I think you'll be more comfortable for your ceremony," she said. I hesitated, and did not answer. She smiled and continued, "You can always change your mind."

We followed Willa into her Zen-like home and up a dark, walnut staircase that wound up and around into a candlelit Upper Room.[2] When we approached the top landing, a painting of a Victorian sword, hanging on the door, jumped out at me. Written below the sword were the words, "*Saint Michael.*" This was the sword I was seeking and I knew what it meant. No random set of circumstances had accidentally brought Michael and me together in that moment. The stranger had been right. Once we committed, a whole stream of unforeseen events that we could not have imagined or planned had taken place.

2. Before we incarnate we use this order to fashion a blueprint which, if we choose to follow it, guides us to unveil and manifest our full potential.

Aristotle taught that everything in nature including humans has function; that nothing is without its purpose. Buddhists call this *dharma*—everything follows its own lawful nature. Let's assume that the lawful nature of our soul is in constant movement over many lifetimes toward greater understanding. In between our lifetimes, like the pause between musical notes, we meet with our spiritual guides and choose the elements of our next life. Together we review our deeds, both good and bad, from previous lives. We look at our strengths, talents, weaknesses, and the issues we need to overcome for our soul's journey toward enlightenment.

Understanding the journey of our soul puts a different perspective on the nature of reality. We choose the body we wish to move around in, the souls we want to incarnate with—our parents, siblings, friends, lovers, partners, and animals. We select the time and place of our birth, and our death, according to the particular astrological aspects of the planets we needed for the journey.[3]

This plan with a purpose, this blueprint, is the hidden order in our lives. By its very nature, it gradually unfolds before us moment to moment. We have the choice to either follow its mysterious pull or to deny it. But we must take responsibility and be accountable for all the realities and experiences we have created.

The basic elements of my blueprint placed my birth—three weeks past my due date—on the coast of North Carolina, during a hurricane. My parents moved to the mountains when I was still an infant, and I grew up playing in the woods with my imaginary friends. The souls I chose as my parents gave me support to manifest my fullest potential. My mother came from a musically talented family. Through her encouragement I learned to appreciate all types of music, and learned to play the piano. But the most important thing she taught me was that it is normal to know things beyond the five senses. My father was Irish-Cherokee. In his quiet manner he taught me respect for others and respect for nature.

Unlike some psychics who had a dysfunctional, traumatic childhood, I did not. My parents loved me immensely, taught me that I could do or be anything I wanted to do or be, and inspired me to be creative. Even though I was an only child, they encouraged my independence. I needed this independence because my mother and father both died before I was twenty years old.

The unveiling of our blueprint does not mean we know our destination. Rather, we sense that "something" is happening through us that is beyond anything we logically know. Author P.M.H. Atwater began researching near-death experiences (NDE) and similar states because of what happened to her during her third near-death experience. In an interview with Atwater, she told me how her blueprint unfolded.

P. M. H. Atwater

After having reached the level where I suddenly, like many NDE experiencers, 'knew all things,' revelations were given to me about the inner workings of creation and consciousness. A voice spoke, I called it the Voice Like None Other because I was familiar with all forms of spirit voices: angel voices, guides, and guardians. This powerful voice was different. My sense was that it was of God. The voice said: "Test revelation. You are to do the research. One book for each death." I was shown what would be in each book. I was not told how long this project would take me or what would be involved. I agreed and consciously chose to return to life. The following year, 1978, I became a researcher of near-death experiences. I have followed the blueprint for my life—my purpose for twenty-four years. To date I have written five books about NDE.

Most of the NDE experiencers I met were through meaningful coincidences. Sometimes I would meet two or three per day. I traveled a lot in my job. A hidden order would frequently give me a lift, unveiling an underlying plan and orderliness to the Universe. For example, one day I was eating lunch at a truck stop near Macon, Georgia. I was seated, reading, and eating at a small table in the middle of the room. A husky truck driver plopped on the empty chair across from me, and before I could say anything, he proceeded to tell me about his near-death experience and the effect it had on him. All I managed to say to him was, "Uh-huh."

It was as if I wore an invisible sign that said, "I am a near-death researcher and I am here to talk to you about your experience." And this is the way it has been since I agreed to my 'contract.' Day and night, no matter where I am—taxi cab drivers, welders, moms with their kids, managers, people in elevators and on the street. All I have to do is appear and smile. The experiencers are waiting for me.

> In the beginning, I had no idea where any of this was going. I just knew that I had to accept this invitation. That's why I came back to life—to do the work.
>
> Synchronicity can't really explain it. There is clearly another force at work, a force or presence that ensures we meet our goal—that we are always in the right place at the right time. That presence continues for me. Certainly, my life is God's Life. That surrender occurred when I died. But, I suspect, there may be another way to regard these experiences—how consciousness works—the presence of spirit when we move into an expanded level of awareness.

As Atwater describes, we may have a destiny, but it appears we also have a choice. What will we do with the situations once they arise? Atwater made a choice to live when death faced her. Or did she? Was the choice already made before she incarnated?

3. Signs of our blueprint are evidenced by meaningful, unusual events.

The mysterious phenomenon of the seemingly accidental meeting of two highly improbable causal chains in a coincidental event has puzzled man for centuries. Carl Jung, best known for his dream analysis and exploration of archetypes of the human psyche, studied this phenomenon and eventually published his thoughts on these types of events in his book *Synchronicity.* Perhaps one of Jung's most significant contributions to the study of human consciousness, *Synchronicity* summarizes his investigation of human connectivity.

As Jung describes, synchronicity has flow and direction. When we are in touch with the flow of a hidden order we experience more meaningful coincidences and a greater awareness of the Universe in which we live. Belleruth Naparstek, author of *Your Sixth Sense*, says, "GOD is a flasher . . . whips open the old raincoat for just a nanosecond and shows ya what's really going on underneath there."

Maybe that flash is the purpose and is meant to catch our attention.

Belleruth related this story of how several highly improbable, unrelated events came together to give her unexpected help.

Belleruth Naparstek

My husband and I were traveling in Israel. We stopped at a Palestinian shop outside of Bethlehem to buy some olivewood carvings and other *chochkes* for our Christian friends. I had piled up a huge stash of goodies but when I reached for my bag, to my chagrin, I saw that I didn't have enough shekels.

I asked the owner, an elderly Arab gent, if he'd please take my check. He looked at me like I was crazy. So I turned to his daughter and asked her. She was reluctant to say no, so she stalled by asking to see the check. . . . I didn't have any with me except for my office checkbook. My office at the time was at 7401 Eastmoreland Road, Suite 327, Annandale, Virginia.

I showed her the checkbook. She looked at it, her mouth dropped, and she ran to her father, yelling in Arabic. He yelled back. They looked incredulous and kept yelling to each other.

It turns out, that very morning they'd put the mother of the family on a plane to go to America to be with her other daughter, who was about to give birth. The daughter lived at 7401 Eastmoreland Road, Annandale, Virginia. She was even on the same floor!

Needless to say, they took my check!

When I got home, and went back to my office, I ran down the hall to say hello. The mother was still there. We had major hugs and laughs.

When "God flashes," it catches our attention! Of all the stores in Bethlehem, why did Belleruth choose the one where the owner had a close link to her office back in Virginia? Could it simply be coincidence?

4. The connecting thread from a hidden order comes about gradually and naturally. It follows its own nature, flowing from our unconscious, our dream states, and our thoughts into the patterns of life.

Creative people often claim that they create their greatest works when they are in this flow—when they are radically transcending their normal consciousness and touching the invisible world. Nietzsche and Wordsworth believed that there is a kind of cognition by which everything happens involuntarily, with a completeness and power beyond ordinary thought. When it comes it is the nearest, most obvious, simplest expression. The great composer Mozart described his experience of this in this way:

> When I am completely myself, entirely alone and of good cheer—say traveling in a carriage, or walking after a good meal, or during the night when I cannot sleep—it is on such occasions that my ideas flow best and most abundantly. Whence and how they come, I know not; nor can I force them. . . .
>
> All this fires my soul, and, provided I am not disturbed, my subject enlarges itself, becomes methodized and defined, and the whole, though it be long, stands almost complete and finished in my mind so that I can survey it, like a fine picture or beautiful statue at a glance. Nor do I hear in my imagination the arts successively, but I hear them, as it were, all at once *gleich alles zusammen*.[4]

The ability to be open to ideas that we have not consciously created, that rise from deep inner-space into our awareness is not limited to famous artists and musicians. Frequently, our dreams bring information we are seeking into our consciousness. Berri Kramer, a mother of four who homeschooled her kids, designed craft kits for *Better Homes and Gardens Magazine* for twenty years. Much of her design work was done in her dreams with a drawing pad and pencils next to the bed. "I rarely remember actually waking up and I never turned on the light, but the designs were ready to be made early in the morning."

The discovery of the *Atocha,* a gold- and silver-laden Spanish galleon that sank three hundred years ago off the Florida Keys, came about because treasure hunter Mel Fisher's son, Dirk, had a vivid dream that the motherlode of the *Atocha* was not where they were presently looking—on a shallow reef—but was near where they had first looked in deeper waters.[5]

It was solely on a gut feeling that I left my life in Norfolk, Virginia, and moved to Providence, Rhode Island. At the time, my now ex-husband did not understand what I was doing, and I could not explain it. I just knew that if I did not change my life, I would die.

My first year in Providence was a year spent asking myself whether I had made the right decision. Where did I think I was going? What was I going to do? Had I made the right decision to leave my life in Norfolk? Should I go back and try to work things out with my husband? In the midst of these uncertainties, I had a series of dreams that supported my decision. First, I dreamt that there was an airplane waiting for me on a runway. Before I could board, I said to no one in particular, "I have to go to my exercise studio." When I reached the studio there was a "Closed" sign nailed across the door. I returned to the airport, walked by the movie star Katherine Ross from *The Graduate,* and boarded the plane. My interpretation of the dream was that there was nothing to work out. I could graduate from that life. The theme song from *The Graduate*, "Mrs. Robinson," told me not only about the life I was leaving—it revealed where I was headed.

The idea of dreams being more than simply our imagination has been around for thousands of years. Many native cultures maintain that only in extraordinary states of consciousness can we be aware of the unseen order, or the inner dreaming of the earth. For example, to the Sng'oi of Malaysia, the dream world is the real world. The world we live in is a shadow world. At night we visit that *real* world, and in the morning we share what we have learned there. We could also say that the *dreamtime* of the Australian Aboriginals is a hidden order making itself known in the world. It tells how the Universe came to be, how human beings were created, and how the Creator intended for humans to function within the cosmos.

5. A hidden order is like the wind. We can only see the effects of the wind, we never see the wind itself.

It would be nice if we could point to our astrological natal chart and say, "Here is the direction my life is going. It is all carefully planned out." But nothing is as easy—or as clear—as we would like it to be. The nudge that pushes us toward our future is frequently silent, invisible, and unexpected.

Al Siebert

Psychologist Al Siebert is the director of the Resiliency Center in Portland, Oregon.[6] We could say his professional journey started when he received a postdoctoral fellowship at the Menninger Foundation. It is a significant honor to be accepted into this program, which allows Fellows a two-year moratorium in which they are free to reexamine and reintegrate their theoretical knowledge and clinical skills. Siebert took this philosophy to heart and asked himself, "Why are mental illnesses so hard to cure?" He also wondered, "Why do most people who want to make the world a better place focus on trying to get other people to change? Why don't they work on themselves?" A series of synchronistic events led Al to getting what he terms his "accelerated postdoctoral education."

> Al's prod toward his surprising destiny came when, against his better judgment, he shared, with his religious wife, his hypothesis about how people with weak self-esteem could free them-

selves from doing things to gain esteem from others. "As far as *I* am concerned," he said, "I am the most valuable person who will ever exist." Appalled, his wife raced to her priest, who told her Al was mentally ill and advised her to contact psychologists and psychiatrists at Menninger.

Several days later the director of training psychology at Menninger telephoned Al and told him that his wife was going to start psychotherapy. He suggested that Al go with her for an interview at the outpatient clinic. Reluctantly, Al agreed.

After a few minutes of superficial talk, the psychiatrist sent Mrs. Siebert down to the waiting room.

"What do you think is upsetting your wife?" he asked.

"Should I be honest with him or should I only tell him what I think he can handle?" Al wondered. He decided that if he had to be deceptive to keep the fellowship, then it wasn't worth having. "It could be some of my ideas," he said, laying out his speculations. "Have you ever realized that when someone says people are trying to force thoughts into his mind, psychiatrists then try to force the thought into the individual's mind that he is mentally ill?"

After listening for a short while the psychiatrist said, "You are mentally ill, Dr. Siebert . . . your thought processes are loose."

"I'm not mentally ill. I'm going through a developmental transformation. It's healthy. I just don't have things sorted out well enough to present them clearly."

"I'm not going to argue. You are mentally ill and need to be in a mental institution. . . . You must go immediately, you are quite sick." Al knew how easy it was for psychiatrists to have someone committed. He reasoned that by going voluntarily, it might be much easier to get out later.

"I spent the first two days, Saturday and Sunday, in treatment for my so-called mental illness on a well-run ward. Monday afternoon I was transferred to the back ward with very deteriorated, warehoused, heavily medicated, chronic patients. The psychiatrists were trying to make me accept that their perception of me was more accurate than my own.

"During the next four weeks I learned more about psychiatry from my 'accelerated post-doctoral education' arranged by the Menninger staff than I would have from two years in their formal program. I experienced first-hand how psychiatric labeling prevents the professional staff from experiencing 'patients' as real people.

"My case conference was held four weeks after my admission. It was already clear to me that the ward doctor couldn't tell I had stopped taking the medication early on. He was playing a doctor/patient game with me that was unrelated to any medical reality. I escaped from the hospital the next day. I had been a voluntary admission so I knew they could not send the police after me. The next morning I called and arranged to come back to the hospital to sign an 'Against Medical Advice' discharge in exchange for my wallet, keys, and watch.

"What I went through closely matches Maslow's (one of the founders of humanistic psychology) description of self-actualizing peak experiences. I was in a state of high consciousness. I knew that everything was happening exactly as it should. It felt joyous to feel my mind breaking free from what Buddhists call 'consensus reality.' My disillusioning, transformation experience was the best thing that ever happened to me."[7]

If our world always operated in a consistent manner, with no place for the unanticipated, Al would probably be a traditional psychologist working with chronic patients in some large psychiatric hospital. There would have been no unexpected turn of events—no effects of a blueprint, propelling him toward his current position. After his experience, Al founded the Resiliency Center in Portland, Oregon and became an advocate for the transformation experience among patients who might otherwise have been labeled mentally ill.[8]

6. Experiencing a hidden order brings an understanding that cannot be put into words. By its very nature it transcends linguistics.

The Gnostics believed that Truth can only be experienced. In Western society we believe just the opposite: we believe that whatever is true has been carefully reasoned out. In our culture, our intellect is deemed most important. Since the early 1800s we have been taught that information comes from books, experts, people from out of town—from any source but our (inner) selves. Many people refuse to believe that it is possible to have knowledge without words or even without thoughts.

One time I experienced a telepathic burst of knowledge, a picture language so dense that each image contained a thousand ideas. If I try to put words to that direct experience I fortunately cannot. Words would only limit the reality of what took place. In my experience knowing and language are separate. Knowing without words, or thoughts, is to know a hidden order through direct experience. It is to sense something beyond our individual self that is the essence of who we are. It is personal contact with our essence, with the voice of Spirit.

7. A hidden order is always present, but without giving it our full attention we miss the opportunity and potential it offers.

Various authors have suggested that we are asleep and need to wake up. We need to cultivate present-moment awareness in order to connect with the unknown, or in order to know our real potential. A.G. Gurdjieff, who spent his life seeking the truth about humanity's existence on Earth, felt that many of the "normal" people we see on the street have been dead for years. He felt they had become joyless automatons who were controlled by mechanical habits of thought, perception, and behavior.[9] Psychologist Charles Tart writes "we are dreaming and entranced—caught in illusions while thinking we are perceiving reality."[10] And Jon Kabat–Zinn contends that we almost willfully ignore the richness of our present moments.[11] When we ignore the present moment we cannot hear the whispers of a hidden order.

If you have ever been in the water with dolphins, you know that if you want to grasp the experience you have to give them your full attention. In fact, if your mind slides into what you want the dolphin to do, or is anywhere but in the present moment, they often leave. A hidden order is similar to spending time with a dolphin. If you don't give it your full attention, you will miss the opportunity that moment in time holds. When it leaves it won't return.

A few years ago we were on a wild dolphin swim in the Bahamas. It had been several hours since we had seen any dolphins, so most of us on board were reading or napping. Will, our good friend and captain of the boat, slipped overboard for a swim and invited me to join him. I declined, but watched as he leisurely swam laps around the 62-foot catamaran. "Come on in, Winter," he called. "The water is perfect."

I smiled and lazily replied, "I'll just watch."

Within moments of my last refusal, eight bottlenose dolphins joined Will and began swimming and playing. This is rare because in the wild bottlenose dolphins are usually shy. Most of our swims were with smaller spotted dolphins. If I had been fully aware I would not have been running on automatic, immediately saying "No" because I was too passive to go for a swim. But I wasn't aware, and so I lost a rare opportunity.

We could say the same for all of our moments. We run on automatic—acting without being present. What opportunities do we miss because we are either remembering the past, thinking about the future, or are simply too impassive to be fully present?

8. The hidden order shows itself to everyone with the same intensity, but only those who are open to shedding preconceived notions about themselves and their reality will consistently see it.

One Sunday morning Eleanor Friede, an editor with Macmillan, was sitting on the deck of her beach house in East Hampton, Long Island, reading a manuscript for a children's book that had been rejected by two dozen publishing houses. "I was totally captured by the images of the story," she said. "I went with it completely and it made me feel wonderful." Suddenly she saw that slim volume, with a jacket of seagulls, in bookstore windows across the entire country.

As Eleanor sensed, *Jonathan Livingston Seagull* was a story for adults, not children. "I felt there were truths in this simple story that would make it an international classic." She adds, "Too many forces came together all at once in the publication of *Jonathan* not to believe in the existence of some kind of a universal information matrix."[12]

What was it about Eleanor Friede that caused her to resonate with *Jonathan Livingston Seagull,* when more than twenty other editors had not?

In the same vein, Spirit showed itself to several, different publishing houses that turned down James Redfield's *Celestine Prophecy*, and J. K. Rowling's *Harry Potter and the Sorcerer's Stone.* Barry Cunningham, who discovered Rowling, originally counseled her to "Get a proper job. . . . You'll never make a lot of money in children's literature."[13] Publishers also told her that the plot, like her sentence construction, was too complex and . . . no one wants to read a story set in a boarding school.[14]

When a hidden order shows itself, by its very nature, we must deviate from the thoughts and actions dictated by others or convention in order to follow it. Eleanor Friede went against others in the publishing industry who thought *Jonathan Livingston Seagull* was a book for children. The book turned out to be wildly successful. It was published in twenty-seven languages and sold over 3.2 million hardcover and 7 million paperback copies. *Celestine Prophecy* became a best-seller, and J.K. Rowling found a publisher, Bloomsbury, and armed with a twelve-thousand-dollar grant from the Scottish Arts

Council, she ploughed into book two, *Harry Potter and the Chamber of Secrets.*

9. Simple, everyday tools help us strengthen the bridge to a hidden order.

In the introduction to *Living the Mindful Life,*[15] Sogyal Rinpoche tells a story about an old woman who came to the Buddha and asked him how to meditate. The Buddha told her to remain mindful, present, and aware of every movement of her hands as she drew water from the well each day, knowing that if she did so, she would soon find herself in the state of alert and spacious calm that is meditation.

One simple tool—paying attention in a specific way—on purpose, nonjudgmentally, in the present moment as we watch the breath, observe nature, sit quietly, drink tea, or explore the *I Ching,* strengthens our connection to a hidden order. Any one of these primary gestures, when given our full attention, can bring us into an awareness of something greater than ourselves. By quieting our mind, removing our awareness from our mechanical habits of thought, we are able to expand beyond our five senses into an inner world and touch the essence of our soul. This is mindfulness. Mindfulness brings awareness that our life has a direction, which unfolds moment by moment.

Experiential Practice

A Hidden Order asks you to consider that there is a hidden design underlying your existence. Because you are Spirit in form, your physical body is the most advanced realization of this hidden, divine potential. Your body is designed to move. Movement displays the unseen language of your soul. Even when you are asleep your body is constantly moving: heart beating, lungs inhaling, cells dividing.

A masterful teacher, your body reflects what is taking place in your mind. It will quickly show you when your are out of balance.

If you desire to connect with the balance and flow of a hidden order, you must have balance in your life and balance in your body, mind, and spirit. Balancing your body with mind and spirit means that you will make every attempt to eat nutritionally balanced meals, and to drink plenty of pure water. You will find a way to relax, to meditate. And you will find a way to move your body, to exercise for its own sake because it is a fundamental expression of being physical, not simply because it is good for you.

There are many paths to reaching this balance. The key is to find the path, and the exercise, that best suits you.

Getting Started

Read the Master Practice, Intention, in chapter 12. Then set your intention to balance body, mind, and spirit as you proceed with the following exercises.

Walking Meditation

> Think of the magic of that foot, comparatively small, upon which your whole weight rests. It's a miracle, and the dance is a celebration of that miracle.
>
> —Martha Graham

Select a place in nature where you can walk slowly, freely, without being observed. This could be an isolated beach, the woods, your living room. It can be anywhere as long as you remind yourself to stay in the moment, taking each step, each breath as it comes. Center yourself. Start walking. Each step should be made as slowly as possible (you may find your balance hard to keep). Be aware of how you shift your weight from one foot to the next, how your heel touches and rolls forward to the ball of your foot just before you push off. Notice how you lift your leg before placing it down.

Walking for Exercise

Walking is an ideal exercise because it is convenient and requires only a good pair of walking shoes.

- Walk (or ride your bicycle) to work, or for errands.
- Give up your riding lawnmower, or the person who takes care of your yard. Use a push mower.
- Take the stairs instead of the elevator.
- Meet a friend for a walk instead of coffee.
- Walk barefoot in freshly cut grass, on a beach, in your living room.
- Walk whenever you can.

Daybook

Journal about your experiences as you moved your body. What happened when you walked in a meditative state? How did you feel after walking instead of riding?

Tool Bag

Attend a yoga class. Yoga is the oldest system of personal development in the world, bringing together body, mind, and spirit. While a class might focus only on getting the physical posture correct, you could find a class flavored with new questions to consider, questions that encourage you to marvel at life's mysteries. Along with the obvious benefits of becoming more flexible, moving more freely, and reducing stress, an added benefit of yoga is that when you are in an asana (a posture that balances the body), you are fully focused on the present moment. Mind and body seem to be one.

Food for Thought

> Few of us have lost our minds, but most of us have long ago lost our bodies.
>
> —Ken Wilbur

Invocation

When you set out to balance your body, mind, and spirit, you are setting a goal that is not immediately visible. You might think this is impossible, but in reality it is only something that, quite probably, you have never thought about. Create a simple invocation asking for help to do what you have never tried.

Ritual

Exercising is always about ritual. Regardless of the activity you choose, a certain amount of preparation is involved. For instance, if you take up yoga, you wear comfortable clothes, hydrate, refrain from eating a large meal before the class, and bring your yoga mat. If you choose walking as your exercise, you will usually set the time and distance that you wish to walk, put on your walking shoes, dress for the weather, and grab a bottle of water. Customarily, at the end of your exercise session you will shower, drink water, and eat a healthy meal. The preparation, the process, the cool-down, the feeling of accomplishment afterward—all of this is ritual.

3
Purpose: When Heaven and Earth Unite

Your vision will become clear only when you look into your heart.

—Carl Jung

Many ancient teachings suggest that we choose to be born, have free will, and a purpose for being here. Their philosophy holds that a progression of lifetimes have resulted in who we are today. For example, Taoists, Buddhists, and Hindus believe that the life we are living now—the degree of happiness, torment, peace, or spiritual awareness—is the result of what we nurtured prior to this incarnation. Similarly, they hold that our present thoughts and decisions determine our future.

Plato's philosophy held a similar view. He wrote that we choose our destiny according to the experiences of our former lives.[1] And tribal groups who have had no contact with the Orient, for example, the Tsalagi Cherokee, think that we must examine visions and thoughts from other lifetimes to discover our purpose and the heart of our own nature.[2]

Although I believe I have lived in other times and places, it is not the idea of being rewarded or punished for past deeds that drives me to discover my purpose. It is an inner longing that says life is a mystery to be lived, not a problem to be solved, and a sense that only I can uniquely translate my life force into action. In the same manner, because you are an original, it is up to you to do what you alone are meant to do on Earth. If you do not use your uniqueness, the world will have lost a source of creativity that cannot be substituted with anything else.

Hermes Trismegistus was the alleged teacher of a system known as Hermetism, of which high magic and alchemy are thought to be twin branches. His *Emerald Tablet* begins, "As above, so below" or, "When Heaven and Earth unite." It continues, "this phrase is thought to hold the key to all mysteries . . . that which is above is the same as that which is below . . . Heaven is the same as Earth . . . the Universe is the same as God, God is the same as man, man is the same as the cell, and so on. All things are born from the same Source."

Heaven and Earth uniting takes place at a personal level when we begin to look at our role in the Universe. . . . Who are we? Why are we here? When we act as if we are separate from Heaven, Earth, and each other, we keep ourselves from realizing our full potential. However, when we understand that we are not separate, both the hidden and the visible, the obscure and the apparent emerge. Heaven and Earth unite.

Our purpose surfaces when hidden signs become visible and direct us toward our future. How we view these signs depends on whether we consider them to be threats or guidance. If we think they are threats, we feel anxious and will often go out of our way to defend and maintain the status quo. But if we see them as guideposts—messages from a hidden order marking our unfolding path—we sense a new freedom and inner peace. We don't have to know where the path will lead, only that if we pay attention we will find our way remarkably well lit.

My precognitive experience and the words of the *I Ching* had both given me ample warning that, like it or not, my destiny was unfolding in a new direction. I just chose to ignore the signs. In my mind, my future—commissioner of mental health—was already shifting toward me. All I had to do was stick with the Office of the Attorney

General, nurture my political contacts, and keep moving in the direction I was headed. But this was all about to change.

I was working on a First Amendment case involving a young, Yale-educated psychiatrist. Every morning he dropped by my office to ask how the case was going. His attitude intimidated me. I had the distinct impression that he did not think I could possibly do an adequate job building his defense without his constant presence. After several weeks of this, I politely informed him that if he did not leave me alone I would not get his, or anyone else's defense prepared.

Three years later, with the trial underway, he raced to catch up with me as I walked toward the federal courthouse. "I understand you hang out at the Quest Bookstore," he said. The Quest carried cutting-edge books on philosophy, UFOs, and psychics. It was one of my private retreat spaces and I didn't readily share that fact, especially not with a hotshot psychiatrist.

I walked faster and did not reply. Not knowing why he asked the question and still intimidated, I didn't want my personal life mixed into my professional reputation. He quickened his pace to keep up and repeated his question not once, but two more times. Finally I snapped back, "So what if I do?"

"So do I," he smiled. "In fact, I carry my lucky tarot card with me." He pulled open his jacket, reached inside, and withdrew the King of Swords tarot card. By now we were inside the federal courthouse, standing in front of the elevator. It was probably a good thing because I was so surprised I could not move. From that moment on we were friends.

A few weeks later he dropped by my office and said, "I think you should meet Mrs. Wrenn, my neighbor."

"Why?"

"She's a psychic. She's interesting."

Over the previous two years I had made an effort to meet every psychic I heard of. A few "knocked my socks off" with their ability to know things about me they had no way of knowing. Others gave me such general information they could have been simply describing what I was wearing that day. I was tired of meeting psychics. "I don't think so. Thanks, anyway."

"She's eighty years old." In fact, she was over ninety.

"Eighty?" That's a lot of experience, I thought. "Give me her number."

A few nights later I called Mrs. Wrenn to schedule an appointment.

"What do you do?" She asked.

"I work in litigation for the attorney general," I replied. "And I am acting issues director for Robin Dalton,[4] who is running for attorney general next year." I paused for a moment before adding, "I also do psychic readings. The process fascinates me. I'm trying to figure out how the ability to 'read' someone works and how the Universe works." As a last thought I added, "and I am a research subject at Monroe Institute labs."

"My dear," she said. "You've got to decide which way you're going to go."

An insight suddenly swept through my total being. Everything in my life stood out very clearly and I knew which way I was not going to go. The following morning I handed in my resignation.

When I stepped away from my job with the state government, it was a step toward a future I could not see. My education and experience were distinctly in the field of mental health: mental illness, mental retardation, substance abuse, and mental health law. How did I expect to leave my stable career and make a living in an elusive field I knew very little about?

Fortunately, not knowing what I was doing has never stopped me from plunging ahead. Over the next few months, I designed a program for drawing out the intuitive process among professional and nonprofessional students.

Six months later I held an introductory workshop in Boston. *Intuitions*, my first book, was not yet in print and I had barely started offering seminars, yet there was standing room only. For me, Heaven and Earth were uniting—my purpose was unfolding.

No matter how we sense the call of a hidden order, the end result is usually the same—we change directions. In the process we must give up our former self, lose our identity, in order to find out who we really are. This can be particularly difficult for men. Just as there is still an underlying expectation that a woman will marry and raise a family—any career she has is secondary to that—a man is expected to be "somebody." He must choose a profession, one that society approves of, stick with it, and make something of himself. When I met Michael, my husband, he was in the process of leaving a prominent position in the corporate world. Although he lacked a clear vision as to where he was headed, he knew that he was not being fulfilled by the way he was investing his time and energy. His story and the ones that follow it clearly show how dramatic, challenging, and rewarding these life changes can be.

Michael Robinson

I took a job on the Gulf oil rigs to repay my college loans, but gave it up in favor of a brief, inharmonious marriage. When the marriage ended, eleven months later, I loaded the totality of my possessions into a tolerably dented 1972 Pinto and drove to Maine where my parents lived. During a brief telephone call, my father had sensed my lack of direction and had offered me refuge. I accepted, less out of relief than because I didn't know where else to go. Later, I learned that aside from wanting to help me in a time of need, he had recognized an opportunity to mend what had, at times, been a trying relationship between us.

An acquaintance of my parents offered me part-time work at the local Coca-Cola plant. I gratefully accepted. I found the new activity intoxicating. And attracted by the potential of increasing monetary rewards, I set my sights on doing whatever was necessary to climb the corporate ladder. Although my starting salary was below the lowest paid secretary, it wasn't long before I worked my way to becoming director of marketing. Enamored with the title and position, and the recognition bestowed upon me by family and friends, Coca-Cola became my mistress. Outwardly, I went from relative obscurity to someone with a respectable image. I felt vibrant—alive. My life was going somewhere. I had purpose.

Ever so slowly, almost imperceptibly, something began to stir just below my awareness. Even though I was surrounded by individuals who were financially and politically successful, something was missing. I had to know what that was. I began to question the path I was on. Is this what life was all about? The business world did not seem to have the answers I was looking for. My interests wandered beyond the boundaries of accepted business protocol. I was drawn to obscure subjects including the workings of the mind, dreams, consciousness, alchemy, and subtle energy. A burning desire to understand what we are doing here began to emerge. What *was* the meaning of life beyond personal gratification? I began to wear distinctive ties.

During this time the principals of our company orchestrated a leveraged buyout and I was offered a small piece of the action. This buyout was to span five years. Enormous profits could be generated by these types of financial schemes so I was part of a once-in-a-lifetime event.

Given my emerging passion, I couldn't regard this potential windfall as significant. Somehow I knew I would not be with the company another five years and I confided this to a friend and co-worker. He knew that a large chunk of money awaited me at the end of five years so his disbelief was understandable. Yet, I was so confident in my prediction that I made a rather large bet with him based on my conviction.

Unexpectedly, the largest stock-market drop in Wall Street

history, Black Monday,[5] occurred soon afterward. The Dow's fall triggered panic selling. A buyer who was willing to pay the five-year projected value of the company emerged and the principals sold for enormous profits. Eleven months into the leveraged buyout I was sitting on a windfall that could sustain my current lifestyle for three years. What a gift—time to contemplate what I was going to do with the rest of my life.

My co-workers expected that I would continue my climb through marketing and sales management in the new corporation, but I knew differently. My time with Coca-Cola was nearing completion—something was compelling me to step out of the cocoon of security.

Innocently, I shared my desire to take reflective time with selected friends and associates. Reception of my idea ranged from the subtle shaking of heads in pity, to those who stridently said it was an act of political suicide to leave a prestigious position without another job. To most, refusing a respectable position in the new company was an act of heresy. They didn't realize I had already left.

Searching for something that has no identity is difficult to understand, let alone explain to others in social circles. This is a real confidence shaker. It was years before I quit introducing myself as, "I was director of marketing for Coca-Cola." Reinventing my self-image beyond what I did or didn't do was a creative challenge.

Now for the part of my story that is most difficult to convey. It's one of those things that you know with certainty, but understanding *why* or *how* you know it remains elusive. Why did I choose the path I did? In reviewing significant events in my life I now see the synchronicity. I took detours which added depth and understanding to my direction. Clearly, there were times when I could have made other choices and my life would have been vastly different—but I didn't. In many cases, though certainly not all, I can see when the choices I made brought frustration and loss. But even distressful events have their place in my present understanding of reality. I see things differently. Decisions I made in the past that I considered productive I now see as somewhat shallow and limited.

How did I get from "there" to "here?" It's not as if one day I suddenly decided to become a more aware human being and voila! Instead, I believe it was my soul whispering through the din of my chattering mind that finally got my attention. This whisper was not in the form of words; rather I was being presented with an unspoken question—a yearning for something more. I began to listen and in so doing, my perspective began to change dramatically.

A global awareness began to emerge in my consciousness. I started to see the world as an integrated whole. Numerous indications suggesting that we are standing on the edge of a major shift in how we view and live in the world became apparent to me. Our current economic system, promoted and protected by our political system, and based largely upon consumption, began to feel outdated. The distribution of wealth and current levels of consumption characterize a world out of balance and there are signs that suggest the Earth can no longer handle the drain on its resources.

The nature of our reality is made of opposites. The pull of opposites is the rhythm of life. When one side becomes stronger or weaker, Nature restores balance by moving in the other direction. We can choose to be cocreators in restoring balance by being open to a shift in consciousness, a greater aspect of humanness—one that is beyond the limitations of the physical self. This consciousness, I believe, is the source of all creativity and innovation. We are an indelible part of this creative flow. My path has become clear. . . . I am an agent of this new consciousness and the restoration of balance.

Susan Griffin-Towbin

Our search for understanding might be easier if our guidance simply sent us a card, maybe when we are seventeen, telling us our purpose in life. Although rare, this can happen, but usually not by mail. A simple question led Susan Griffin-Towbin, a Canadian journalist, to her purpose.

> "Let me put my story in context," Susan said as she sat at our kitchen table and sipped tea. "I was brought up in a family where there was absolutely no religion. You can say I was reared in the Church of Golf. When I was twenty-one I was hospitalized and became deathly ill. I was in an isolation ward for two and a half months due to a misdiagnosed burst abscess in one of my fallopian tubes. When it ruptured, it caused acute peritonitis, poisoning my whole abdominal cavity. I was in so much pain for so long that I really wanted to die. I was toxic and the suffering was unrelenting. Morphine didn't touch the pain. Even in my dreams I begged the nurses to please let me die.
>
> "During one of these days, I had a vision that I was in a great hall, lying on the bottom of an empty swimming pool that looked like a Roman bath. Around the bath were ordinary, white marble columns that supported the ceiling. Two steps led down to the pool. I wanted to die and was praying that I would.
>
> "I was wrapped tightly, in white sheets like a mummy, just like I was in the hospital. I was so weak, all I could move was my eyes. Suddenly, everything became more intense because . . . the Rolling Stones were going to have a concert in that hall. I knew I would be trampled to death.
>
> "While I was having these thoughts, I noticed the wall at the foot of my bed. I thought I caught a glimpse of a pink or pastel blue color, like a reflection of a rainbow. It pulled my attention. What was that? My watching seemed to animate the color. The more I looked, the more intense the color became. Not only were the colors bright, they began to take on form,

changing into a large mural on the wall. I was still in pain, but I was totally focused and fascinated by what was taking place in front of me.

"The colors folded into a Shangri-la scene with tropical birds, animals, and fruit. It was very lush and beautiful. Everything was in a state of perfection. The painting continued to change, taking on more dimensionality. It took on textures, like a tapestry, transformed itself into a sculpted relief, and then moved out from the wall. I was reminded of looking through an old 3-D viewer—except this was real. A lush rainforest appeared. In the center of the forest was a huge cross made of branches, not flat wood, but small trees.

"A man was nailed to the cross. It was not an idealized, romanticized Christ figure—it was Jesus. His arms were outstretched. I didn't have my usual, two-dimensional vision because I could see around him, the curve and sides of his arms. He wasn't dead, but he didn't look straight at me. His eyes held an expression I have never seen before—absolute agony combined with total surrender. He was definitely suffering, but he was not fighting it. He knew that even though it was horrible, it was exactly the way it had to be. I heard a very neutral voice inside my head ask me a question.

"'You think you've suffered?' There was no bias or judgment from the voice. It wasn't 'You think *you've* suffered?'

"When I heard that question every emotion I have ever experienced occurred simultaneously. I felt shame, joy, relief, guilt, and I had a total understanding of everything in the world. I realized that I had given up way too soon. I knew that if I answered the question, 'Yes,' I would be allowed to die and all the suffering would stop. Dying wouldn't be the end, but I would be allowed to get out of my physical body. And if I said 'No,' I would continue to live, but there would be no relief. The pain would return immediately and I would be right back in the life I was in. Nothing would have changed.

"But because of what I saw and the rush of emotion I experienced, I knew that I could handle way more. I had so grossly underestimated myself it was unbelievable. In that moment I knew I had just barely begun my life—there was something I needed to do. And, for a second, I knew what it was. My purpose was intensely clear. For a second. The quality of what I felt was so tangible and real I didn't need to remember what my purpose was—I knew I would fulfill it.

"Over the years I have come to believe that my purpose is to connect with people, to court their spiritual opening. Everyone has all the information they need inside of themselves—I am here to support that."

Most people have not decided what they really want in life. Once that decision is made, in all likelihood it will require a change, and change is frightening. Change, by its nature, isn't predictable. Part of the change is that, like Michael, we have to give up our sense of who we are, our personal history, and our familiar identity. We may not like the life we are living, but we still will use tremendous energy to deny that creative part of us that wants change. It can be easier on some levels to live a life that is not creative. So how do you discover your path? You may find the answer surprising: You don't. Your path finds you. I believe that a primal directive propels us to our destinies, regardless of what our reasoning minds tell us.

What are your desires and longings? Let them take you out into the world, one step at a time, starting right now. Your next step is the only one you can take right now. Deep down we all want to make a difference for having lived this lifetime. Elisabeth Kubler-Ross says that when we reach the pearly gates of heaven we are asked just two questions: "What did you contribute?" And "How much of your potential did you use?" It is never too late to start and you are never too old to make a difference.

Experiential Practice

Before knowing your purpose you need to know who you are—your abilities, talents, limitations, fears, self-image—in essence, your blueprint. The daybook, invocation, bath and rhythm rituals that follow are designed to help you discover your mission.

Getting Started

Begin with the Master Practice in chapter 9, Ego and Beliefs, because almost all of your limitations are beliefs that you hold and they may be preventing you from discovering your purpose. Then continue on with the exercises below.

Daybook

You have to know where you have come from in order to know where you are going. This exercise will help you find out what you have created in this life. We will start with a self-analysis exercise. Take a few minutes to fill out this analysis of yourself. Laying out the simple facts of your life can help you discover the purpose that is awaiting you.

Physical Body

Describe yourself as simply and objectively as you can. Be honest; this worksheet is meant for you alone.

Physique (height, weight, eyes, ears, body build)
Senses (Intuitive? Strong sense of smell, touch? Good eyesight?)
Health
Personality
Limitations/Challenges
Talents/Abilities

Purpose

Birth date, place
Location of home you grew up in, type of surroundings (rural, urban)

Parents (strengths, weaknesses, talents, passions, interests)
Your interests
Unexpected surprises/events in your life
Who do you respect? Why?
What do you value? Why?
Present environment (urban/natural)
Dreams
Fears
Chosen career
What gives you satisfaction?
What do you avoid?
What comes easily? What gifts readily manifest?
Where do you feel comfortable?
What is missing in your life?
You came into this life to do what?
To accomplish what?

After answering the above questions, reflect on what you see as major turning points. Behind every major turning point in your life lies a hidden order. Now look over all of your responses and answer the following questions for each one.

- What were the major turning points in your life?
- What direction did each point to?

Tool Bag

Judgments are the part of our belief system that labels something as good or bad. Our tendency to label usually elicits an emotion: love, tenderness, anger, fear, jealousy. Instead of judging, consider measuring your preferences. Measuring has no emotional bias and can lead to understanding. What we measure simply is . . . tall, short, dark, light, etc. Spend the day without judging anything.

Food for Thought

> If a man does not keep pace with his companions, perhaps it is because he hears a different drummer. Let him step to the music which he hears, however measured or far away.
>
> —Henry David Thoreau

Invocation

Stand or sit comfortably with your feet slightly apart. Let your arms hang loosely at your sides but not touch your body, or fold them into your lap, palms facing up. Take a deep breath and as you inhale, imagine a white light coming into the top of your head. As you exhale, release anything that no longer serves you.

Because this invocation is for clarity and finding your purpose, it will hold more power if you make it as clear as you can. Use the following guidelines:

- State your name.
- Call up your highest Source of Light and Truth. This may be your higher self, God, the goddess, Allah, the One, Clear Consciousness.
- If you like, you can also ask for the assistance of your guides, angels, masters, and loved ones in spirit.
- Then ask for whatever help you desire in finding your purpose. You might ask for clarity, to see through your limitations, to see the true essence of yourself.
- Repeat the invocation three times.

Here is an example:

> Guardians, Ancient Ones, draw near.
> Bless, protect, my sight make clear.
> East and South, North and West,
> I drop all image and pretense.
> Limitations now dissolve,
> My highest potential to evolve.

Ritual

We use ritual as a tool for transformation. The following bathing rituals serve two purposes: to help you release your personal limitations and to bring clarity to your gifts. The music ritual will help you sense your body rhythm and the rhythm of your life.

You will need:

Privacy of a bath
Sea or bath salts
Candles
Herbs

Choose your herbs according to their symbolic import:

Orange: confidence, hope, joy—use the peel or zest of fresh or dried orange, essential oils, or incense

Lavender: peace, conscious mind—use fresh or dried flowers, essential oils, or incense

Once you have selected your herbs, tie a small amount in a square of cheesecloth or muslin like a big tea bag.

Bath Ritual 1

Try to perform this ritual on a waning moon, when the moon is decreasing from the full to crescent, close to midnight. Remember that intent is everything, so if you are unable to wait for a waning moon, or for midnight, *intend* to create the optimum conditions. Prepare the space by clearing the bathroom of unwanted clutter, dirty clothes, magazines, makeup, or toiletries you no longer use. This is all excess baggage, holding you to the energy of the past. Clean the mirrors, tub, and toilet. Use candles for your only light. Place one candle at the foot of the tub where you can see it as you soak.

Run a warm bath. When the tub is half full sprinkle the bath salts into the water, then slip into the bath. Allow your body to relax.

Repeat your invocation, imagining that the "former you" is dissolving in the water, taking with it any limiting beliefs, worries, or concerns. When you sense that the ritual is complete, let the water drain out while you remain in the tub. Rinse or shower off. Pat dry. Put out the candles. Thank the divine and the spirits.

Now that you have begun to consciously seek your purpose, it is important that you pay attention. This first bathing ritual marks a crossroads in your life. In the days and weeks that follow this first bathing ritual, view every experience as significant and pay attention as they will be bringing you information about your purpose.

Bath Ritual 2

The new or waxing moon is the best time for this ritual, again, close to midnight. Your bathroom should have remained uncluttered. Place a candle at the foot of the tub, and another so that it lights the mirror. Run a warm bath, add your orange and lavender herbs, and slip into the water. Allow your body to relax. Repeat your invocation, imagining a white light flowing into the top of your head, bringing with it a heightened awareness of your talents, insights, and gifts. When you sense that the ritual is complete, climb out of the tub. Pat dry. Put out the candles. Thank your Source of help and guidance.

Finding the Rhythm of Your Life Ritual

You will need:

A place where you can play music as loudly or as softly as you like
A CD or tape player
A variety of music

It would be impossible for me to write about a hidden order, blueprint, or ritual without including music. Most of my rituals revolve around music. Even if I am performing a bathing ritual, I will have music playing. I often listen to music to relax, to write, to set my mind for a specific talk, and to guide clients into their innermost selves. I also use it to move into an expanded space when I do medical readings.

In his book, *Drumming at the Edge of Magic,* Mickey Hart quotes John Blacking as saying, "Music is given to us with the sole purpose of establishing an order in things, including the coordination between man and time."[6]

Joachim-Ernst Berendt, a German jazz historian, proposed that (a) since the one sure thing we can say about fundamental matter is that it is vibrating and (b) since all vibrations are theoretically sound, then (c) it is not unreasonable to suggest that the Universe is music and should be perceived as such.[7] This would support Pythagoras, the Greek mathematician and mystic, when he said "A stone is frozen music."

I believe that Berendt is right—the Universe is music. I believe that we catch glimpses of our blueprint, or hidden order, when we are in the "space between the notes."

This ritual is about finding the rhythm that goes with how you feel and what you are thinking. When you are in touch with the rhythm of your body, you are in touch with the rhythm of life, of your purpose. I suggest that you select a piece of music, sit or lie down, and just listen. If the music is loud, lie on the floor.

Lewis Thomas, biologist and writer, suggests that:

> Music is the effort we make to explain to ourselves how the mind works. . . . If you want, as an experiment, to hear the whole mind working, put on *St. Matthew Passion* and turn the volume all the way up. That is the sound of the whole central nervous system of human beings, all at once.

Or you can listen to the sound of the Aboriginal didgeridoo, such as Baka's *Outback* CD. Experiment.

4
Health: Nourishing the Body, Mind, and Spirit

May you live all the days of your life.

—Jonathan Swift

The idea that we cannot heal the body without the cooperation of the mind is a familiar one. "I am responsible for the creation of my health—at some level I participated in the creation of this illness and I can participate in the healing of it." This philosophy has made its way into mainstream consciousness over the past decade. What was once regarded as New Age speculation is now current wisdom. Worries that we carry around express themselves in wrinkles and frown lines; burdens or added responsibilities are likely to show up as back or shoulder aches; and people or problems you can't stomach become ulcers, gastritis, or colitis.

Consider the possibility that our health and general well-being is not just about our attitudes, memories, and beliefs but also about something much more. Beyond the mind-body connection, an organizing principle continually nudges us to be the men and women we are capable of being—body, mind, *and spirit.* It ceaselessly whispers suggestions for healing and maintaining this remarkable vehicle that our soul rides around in.

Usually we think these whispers are just our thoughts, arising from what we think we "should" be doing. But when the thoughts appear spontaneously and unbidden, with no judgment about the outcome, we had best pay attention. A hidden order is creating a longing inside of us, a yearning to first find the courage to seek and then face *our* Truth. If we ignore this yearning, that gentle tap on our shoulder may turn into the boulder that drops on our head.

Toward the end of my former marriage, I started sleeping on the extreme edge of our king-size bed. If I turned over, I would fall onto the floor. One morning I rolled to the floor with one clear thought going through my mind, "If I don't leave this life, I'm going to die." I spent the next week scrutinizing my life, my external circumstances, and my internal feelings about it. The truth was vividly reflected in where I slept—I had moved to the edge. It was time to leap. On the deepest level, I knew I already had.

That same quiet voice has whispered "yoga" most of my adult life. My standard response was, "I know I am not flexible and yoga would be good for me, but . . ." I would list a thousand reasons why I could not take up yoga at that time, telling myself that I would in the future.

Then the voice made another statement. It did not say that I needed to practice yoga or "else," it just whispered "yoga." Fortunately, guidance is patient. If we ignore a suggestion, it will find another, usually more vocal way to get the information across—sometimes it sends a messenger. The whispers of "yoga" moved into my dreams when a blue-eyed Indian guru, dressed in running clothes, appeared. We never spoke, but an understanding beyond words passed between us. Still, I did not take up yoga.

Quite unexpectedly, a friend gave me two basic yoga tapes. I put them aside after looking at them once. Two weeks later she brought me a third yoga video—*Inhale, with Steve Ross.* I popped it into the video player and was immediately hooked on yoga. Am I more flexible? Yes. More balanced? Most definitely. More importantly, during a recent meditation "the breath breathed me." This sense of being the breath, not separate from it is a result of my practice of yoga. The whispers, dreams, and the messenger were all forms of inner guidance telling me what my body needed.

Real-life messengers who appear on our path may be total strangers. Their only purpose in our lives may be to get us to hear the whisper of a hidden order—as it was in the case of Sally Spangler.

Sally Spangler

Sally Spangler, a nurse anesthetist, hit job burnout. She was aware of the internal and external pressures she was under and of their effects on her body. What she was not aware of was that her illness was the Universe giving her a gentle tap. Her search for healing pointed her toward her mission in life.

> I developed severe, unrelenting heartburn and gastroesophageal reflux disease that did not respond to medication. Yes, there was something that I could not "stomach." Knowing my internist would suggest surgery as the next step, I began a desperate search for an alternative. I suddenly thought of a paper I had written on acupuncture anesthesia years earlier. A little footwork and research led me to an acupuncturist in the city where I worked. During the course of treatments, I realized my life was seriously out of balance. I wanted to prevent illness now—not just in myself but also in others—rather than try to fix people after the damage had already taken place, as I had been doing in my profession for thirty years. Feeling it was hopeless to make a career change at age fifty, I fell into a deep depression.
>
> One morning, after working a twelve-hour night shift, I drove my mother to her church. When I dropped her off, I realized I was very sleepy. A nap in the church sanctuary seemed like a good idea. Although I awoke feeling refreshed, there was a circular, buzzing vibration in my chest. As my eyes cleared, I saw a mirage in front of me—a brilliant, coral sun rising over a mist-covered blue mountain and lake. A quiet, matter-of-fact voice said, "*You* should do acupuncture." The scene quickly faded. I

stood to leave and looked back over my head. There, hidden in the dimness, was a picture of a rainbow with the words: "God's promises are forever."

Uncertain about this experience, I kept it secret. My heartburn returned and again I sought out acupuncture. This time I found an excellent acupuncturist locally. During treatment I was internally prompted to ask him to recommend acupuncture schools, which he did. Subsequently, I contacted the school he recommended, which turned out to be exactly what I wanted. I joined the class in late December, caught up on the work of the fall semester, and passed all the midterm exams on time. Without a doubt this was the career I was meant to have. It nurtures me.

In this story we see the effects of an underlying pattern that quietly and subtly shapes lives, going well beyond maintaining the health of the body. During the process of conducting thousands of intuitive readings, I have not been able to ignore that there is some divine orchestrating principle that is responsible for the subtle energy, the physical body, and the issues that we bring into this life.

When I am doing an intuitive "body scan," or a reading, which I always do from a distance, I use my internal vision and my felt sense to assess this field surrounding the client's physical body and the chi, or subtle energy, flowing in and through their body.[1] I sense the energy field as being luminous and egg-shaped, containing everything that I need to know about the client.If I sense an imbalance in the field or in the flow of chi, the client is possibly sensing inner stress. Because disease will appear in the energy body before it manifests the physical body, the client has the opportunity to address the causes of their stress.

Once I begin a reading, the information continually unfolds—moving from the densest physical levels to the lightest Spirit. Energy closest to and in the client's body—the "body consciousness"—tells me about the health of the body.

While I am exploring the physical body of the client, my

awareness automatically expands into the emotional "ego consciousness" energy field. (It is my belief that the body resides within the soul, not the other way around.) If the client is holding fear, anger, or guilt, or if they have a "broken heart," that vibration will be contained in their emotional field, and eventually show up as illness or emotional distress in the physical body. When individuals become aware that what they are thinking is taking form in the body, they can change their thinking to prevent this from occurring.

The idea that our health is a result of more than our genes and our conscious mind is demonstrated in a medical reading that I did several years ago for a young woman I'll call Nancy, a pianist. Nancy had numerous physical complications including temporal lobe epilepsy and slurred speech resulting from her medication. Her hands were so twisted that she was unable to play the piano. She was certain she had a brain tumor, but I knew that that was not the case. In the reading, I told her she was turning her energy inward on herself, that she had given up her personal power, and was seeing herself as a victim. She kept asking to meet me in person, but I felt there was nothing more I could tell her.

Her therapist finally encouraged me to see her, so reluctantly, I agreed to meet her with her neuropsychologist and the physician who was my monitor at the time. I remember sitting beside her on the sofa, feeling my mind was totally blank. Then a voice spoke in my head, it said, "Heal her."

To which I quickly replied, "I don't do healings."

"Heal her."

I looked over at Nancy, her hands rolled into tight fists, her speech so slurred she was difficult to understand, still holding on to her belief that she had a brain tumor.

"Couldn't you give me someone easy?" I asked. "Have you looked at her? She'll be hard."

"Heal her."

I turned to Nancy and repeated what I had said in the reading, "I can feel your energy turning in on you. If you want to get better you have to reverse its direction."

As I spoke a picture formed in my head, so I continued. "I see you as a Japanese man. You let your nails grow so long in that life they pierced the palms of your hands. Unable to use your hands, you had to be served by others."

Nancy's face turned ashen. At first I thought she was angry with me for suggesting such a thing, but at last she spoke, "Oh, my God! I saw that life when I underwent hypnosis, trying to uncover the reasons for my physical disabilities." She finished the story, adding details she remembered from her session. It is not important whether Nancy believed that was really her past life, or whether it was simply a symbolic representation of her current situation. The important thing is what we do with the information. How can it help us see our present circumstances more clearly?

Our meeting ended and we said our goodbyes.

Two weeks later, I received a call from the physician I worked with. "You heard what happened to Nancy?"

"Oh, God!" I whispered hoarsely, "She died."

"She got well."

Nancy usually wore splints to bed at night in an attempt to straighten out her hands. After our meeting she "forgot" to put her splints on. When she awoke her hands and speech were normal.

You may think I am telling you this story to show a miraculous healing. Yes, three of us—a physician who was a Quaker,[2] a neuropsychologist, and myself—were gathered with the purest of intentions to help Nancy get well. And my experience has been that there is power when three or more are gathered. The healing that occurred was a combination of all of our energy, and especially that of Nancy herself, who took the information and "ran with it."

But her healing is not why I am telling you this story. Nancy's story is really about how our attitudes and belief systems affect us. This story does not end with Nancy returning to her career as a pianist. Her neuropsychologist wanted her to meet with me one more time. Six weeks later, on the way to our meeting, Nancy was in a car accident. She was driving. All of her symptoms returned.

We have to ask what beliefs she held that would not let her heal permanently? How did her disabilities serve her? Where does a hidden order fit into her life?

I believe that, at a deeper level, Nancy had an agreement with the three of us to come into her life. What we did once we met was a choice. She created her healing as a challenge and an opportunity to reflect on the life she was creating. She was meant to remember that we are more than body and mind, we are also spirit. She unconsciously aligned with a hidden order when she forgot her splints and, for a moment, touched the underlying pattern of her life, which was to stay healthy and well.

Every personal challenge or mishap we encounter gives us another opportunity to take stock of what we are creating in our life. For reasons only Nancy knows, she was not ready to embrace her healing.

It is my belief that when we create our lives we do not elect to contract a specific illness such as AIDS or a brain dysfunction like temporal lobe epilepsy. What we choose are our biological parents, our environment, our particular subtle energies, strengths, skills, and talents. We create opportunities to confront ourselves, which force us to see beyond the veil that separates body, mind, and spirit. We plan challenges that push us to take responsibility for our lives. Then we make agreements with other souls to cross our paths; and we make agreements with ourselves to listen and watch for the signs of our life's design.

We have chosen to be here now, to be alive when global warming is an immense threat not only to the environment, but to all life; when science is God and "better living through chemicals"—perfectly manicured lawns, pills to lower our cholesterol and increase our sex drive—are facts of life; when enormous electromagnetic fields circle the earth; and when we have polluted much of the surface water on the planet.

Healing our body of the flu can be arduous. But the idea of rectifying global warming seems overwhelming for one person to undertake, until we look at Larry Dossey's research on the transpersonal effects of the mind and the power of prayer.[3] His results suggest that our mind may affect not just our body, but also the body of another person at a distance, even when that distant individual is unaware of the effort being made on their behalf. This concept has huge implications individually, and on our potential to solve the ills of the world. It means we are not mutually exclusive. We are part of an underlying, evolving order of life that coexists, overlaps, and works together to create reality.

Little by little, if we can believe that we are responsible for the creation of our health, then we must also believe we are responsible for the co-creation of the environment, and of the disharmony in the world. When we move from believing to knowing, when our fears dissolve, directing us to action for the good of the whole, a hidden order has wrapped us in its arms.

Experiential Practice

Because this chapter is on health, I ask you to focus on your belief systems around health, wellness, disease, and preventive maintenance. Underlying core beliefs and checking your attitude about life can either support you in wellness, or undermine any attempts that you might make to create health.

I have included what I believe to be essential ingredients for the creation of wellness: discovering, sensing, and moving chi, and asking for forgiveness for self and others. The chapter closes with a healthy green-tea ritual.

Getting Started

Once again, I am referring you to the Master Practice exercise, Ego and Beliefs in chapter 9. Please review it and then continue on with the exercises below.

Daybook

If you want your life to start moving in the direction of your choice, you must know what beliefs support where you stand now. This exercise is designed to help you consciously see the truth about your life and begin to understand the supporting ideas on which your current decisions are based. It will help you understand your beliefs and review your internal circumstances.

Begin with an internal review of what you believe to be true, with what we can call your core beliefs. They can be in any area—love, money, sex, religion, politics, and so on. These beliefs form your perspective on how the world operates, and may become self-fulfilling prophecies.

Then write down ten of these beliefs and underneath each one, put down the reason you are convinced it is true. Ask yourself what part of this belief is a true description of reality? What do you personally know to be true? Have you tested this belief or have you simply accepted it on some other authority as true?

Next, write down ten things that you do not believe in, and why you do not believe in them. Ask yourself which part of each belief is a true description of reality. What do you personally know to be true? Have you tested these beliefs or have you simply accepted them on some other authority as true?

Finally, identify some of our cultural, mass-conscious beliefs. How do these beliefs serve us? How do they get in the way?

When you finish identifying the beliefs above, ask yourself this question: How many of your beliefs did you consciously choose? Journal your thoughts, feelings, and discoveries.

Attitude

Our attitude is made up of a mental position, feeling, or emotion in response to a fact or state. Take stock of your attitudes. Is the glass half-empty or half-full? Are you generally optimistic and upbeat? Do you hold the opinion that things will get better or do you feel the world is falling apart and that there is nothing you can do? What beliefs support your attitude? Write them in your journal.

Memories

Our memories, our early childhood experiences, and occasionally past life experiences, such as the one Nancy describes in the story on page xx, distract us from the present moment. The present moment is where all healing and all creativity take place. The more attention we give to the past, the more we empower and energize it, letting it dictate who we think we are. On a simple level, we repeat the way we catch a cold or the flu because we draw up a memory of "how it works," how we always catch colds. Even a positive memory takes us from the present moment. We daydream about a first love, a trip to New York or Paris, high school friends. When we are lost in our memories there is no room for anything new to enter. What memories are keeping you from hearing how to nourish your body, mind, and spirit?

Tool Bag

The tool here is subtle energy. Subtle energy is a concept that is hard to define within our current scientific paradigm because it is difficult to measure using conventional instrumentation. Described by many ancient traditions as chi, ki, prana, etheric energy, orgone, mana, or homeopathic resonance, it is traditionally accepted that expansions of consciousness often are related to changes in subtle energies.

Nourishing our body, mind, and spirit takes action. We need to pay attention to the subtle energy around us, acting on what it tells us. Feng shui expert Nancy SantoPietro[4] suggests that the environment around us is full of clues that alert us to potential health problems. Our role is to decipher the clues, which appear first as subtle energy, and make changes if necessary.

Subtle energy is a light, breezelike force that we can all learn to perceive. Right now, be aware of how you feel. Do you feel calm, alert, excited, tense, relaxed? The next time you find yourself in a group of people notice how you feel.

Subtle energy travels up and down the spine. Sit up, have good posture, notice how your energy level changes. Do you feel more alert, more aware? Our breath moves this subtle energy in and out of our body, awakening our body's center of power. Try this experiment: Take a deep breath, breathe all the way down into your belly and diaphragm. Your stomach should push out as you inhale. Breathe in pure light energy and let it travel down your spine and flow out, back into the earth.

Now, hold your hands about two to five inches apart, palms facing each other. Close your eyes. What do you feel? Move them back and forth, closer, farther. This energy is very subtle. You may experience it as heat. Imagine creating a ball of energy between your hands. Can you feel it? Slowly bring your hands back together until you feel a slight pressure, like a magnet. Hold your dominant hand one arm's length in front of your face with the palm facing you. Close your eyes. Slowly bring your palm toward your face. What do you notice?

For the purpose of understanding subtle energy and its effects on the body, we will focus on the three energy fields that are closest to the body: emotional, mental, and spiritual. They are the densest and easiest to recognize. Each layer is a body. They are all alive and functioning, and all the distinct layers are interconnected. Imbalance or disease will show up in the energy fields before actually appearing in the physical body. Said another way, the physical body manifests the state of the energy bodies.

Experiment sensing subtle energy with another person. Hold your dominant hand about three feet from their head. Close your eyes.

Slowly bring your hand toward their head. Stop when you sense a change in energy. See where your hand is, then proceed. Remain at least four to six inches from their head. Otherwise, you will end up in their physical body energy field. If you get too close you won't be able to distinguish the energy.

Next, stand one arm's length behind your partner. Hold your palms about four inches from their back. Slowly move your hands down the back of their head, back, and legs. It is important to remember to always move in a downward motion, not upward. What do you notice? Move to the front and do the same thing.

After working with your partner, tell them what you felt and ask for any feedback they can give you. For example, if your hands felt hot or cold as you moved down their right arm, they may have broken that arm during childhood. Or, you may also have picked up an energy block that is not showing up on the physical body at this time. Feedback is critical because it is important to be aware that you can misinterpret the information. Its purpose is not to grade how you did, but to help you understand the ways you receive information, the origins of your thoughts and images during the session.

Some people scan their pets in the same way. Be aware that some animals do not like to have their energy field scanned. If you are scanning an animal, make sure that you touch the animal from time to time and that you stop if the animal becomes agitated or restless.

The following exercise is one of my favorites. I learned how sensitive I am to electrical poles and wires from this experience.

Be sure to pay attention to *all* of your senses during this exercise. Have a friend lead you blindfolded around your yard or a park. Then hold your palms facing each other and have your friend place objects between your hands. Do not touch the objects. Say any adjective that comes to mind, for example: long, brown, thin, sharp. Do not use nouns, even if you think you know what the object is. A noun will lock onto a picture and close out any additional information. Have the friend lead you to a tree, a person, or an animal. What do you notice? When you have finished have the friend show you the things you experienced non-visually while you were blindfolded. Take a break, switch roles and repeat the exercise.

Now that you have a feel for subtle energy, it is time to review your external circumstances. This time you will consciously sense the energy of your immediate surroundings. Begin the same way as when you learned to sense energy: close your eyes, take a deep breath, breathe in energy, let it travel down your spine and flow back into the earth. Sense the people around you. Do you feel more energetic around some people than others? Do you feel more drained or tired around certain people, but not others?

One of the best places to get in touch with your external environment is in your own home. You have probably, over time, acclimated to your surroundings and you literally do not see what is there. Use all of your senses in each area of your living space to get a sense of the subtle energy.

What life is in your home, what grows or cannot grow outside? Do you have pets? Plants? Walk through each room of your home. Stand still, close your eyes. How do you feel? Open your eyes. What do they fall on? Is this something you need to change?

Now scan your greater surroundings. Have you experienced any spiritual or mystical occurrences that suggest that you are living in the ideal space for you at this time? Or have you experienced something that seems to be advising you to move, insinuating that where you live isn't healthy? Are you never able to feel stable where you live? What buildings, businesses, or places of worship or burial are close by? What electromagnetic energy fields, high-tension wires are near?[5] We are just beginning to research the effects of electromagnetic energy on individuals who are exposed to it on a regular basis. Consider these and other related questions. Take stock of your surroundings and their effects on your well-being.

Food for Thought

> If you want to see what your body will look like tomorrow, look at your thoughts today.
>
> —Navajo saying

Invocation

We use prayer as an active way to communicate with Source, usually making a request or asking a question, although it could simply be giving thanks. Some say that prayer is when we are speaking to Source, and meditation, or our intuition, is when we are listening.

This Buddhist Metta Prayer of Forgiveness is based on having a generous heart that wishes happiness to all beings, as well as to oneself. Because lovingkindess comes from the benevolence of our heart, and does not depend on people or conditions having to be a certain way, it does not easily change into anger or bad feelings.

Sit quietly and center yourself. Follow your breath. Then recite:

> May I be forgiven for all offenses that I have committed . . .
> Knowingly and unknowingly . . . by thought, word, and deed . . .
> May I be forgiven for them all.
>
> May I forgive all those who have offended me . . . Knowingly and unknowingly . . . by thought, word, or deed . . . May I forgive them all.
>
> May I be well and happy . . . free of suffering and pain . . . liberated.

Ritual

In this ritual you will focus your attention on the process of brewing and serving green tea in order to create health. The objective of this green-tea ritual is for you to live in the present moment and to be mindful of your breath. Yogis tell us that we breathe 21,647 times a day. How many of these breaths are you aware of?

The entire ritual is designed to focus the senses so that you are totally involved in the process and not distracted by mundane thoughts. Deeply rooted in Chinese Zen philosophy, it is a way for you to remove yourself from the routine affairs of day-to-day living and to achieve, if only for a time, serenity and inner peace. This inner peace is the path to wellness.

In *The Book of Green Tea*, Diana Rosen describes her relationship with tea in the following manner:

> Tea is a retreat in a cup. Tea is quite literally "therapy in a cup," a way to sort out, think through, resolve to do. Tea gives you permission to relax, to be in the moment, and to be truly who you are. . . . Tea is the most intimate of beverages. To truly appreciate tea, you need to sit down and be introspective. Within moments, you will have greater clarity of thought and a clearer sense of purpose. It is just you, your thoughts, and the magic of a bowl of tea.[6]

There are many physical reasons to drink green tea. Numerous scientific studies indicate that the antioxidants in green tea keep you healthy—they may lower your risk of cancer, fight heart attack and stroke, prevent tooth decay, calm you down, improve joint mobility, help heal skin damage, and, because it counters bad breath better than mint, parsley, or chewing gum, green tea can be good for your social life.[7]

The basic rules for preparing tea are to buy well, use pure spring water at the right temperature, and brew it in a vessel that is appropriate to the tea itself. Follow these instructions and you will begin to appreciate for yourself the fine art of tea.

Selecting Your Tea

It is that search for the perfect cup of tea that keeps tea-making so interesting. Sencha is one of my favorites. The dark loden green, grasslike leaves brew up into a delicate liquid that is grassy sweet and astringent. There are numerous grades of sencha and even the mediocre ones can be wonderful. I have listed some sources for tea in the Resources section of this book.

Brewing

Choose a teapot that is small and preferably porcelain. First, warm your teapot with hot water and empty it. Then, fill your kettle with fresh, cold spring water. It is important to use fresh water as reboiled water contains less oxygen. Measure a teaspoon of tea for each cup and place it in the pot. Add an additional teaspoon for stronger tea. When you see the steam coming out of the kettle, pour water over the loose tea. Pour about a cup more water than you will drink into the pot. Black teas should steep for three to five minutes in water brought to just below a boil. Green and white teas should steep in cooler water, barely steaming, for two minutes or less. Sencha is uniquely rich in vitamin C, and may be infused several times.

As you brew the tea, allow yourself to think only of the process, being mindful of your breath and every motion. Let your intention be to cleanse the six senses from impurities.

5
Love and Relationships: Mutual Attraction

I seem to have loved you in numberless forms, numberless times, in life after life, in age after age forever.

—Rabindranath Tagore

The wisdom of the *I Ching* speaks of relationship in terms of mutual attraction: "Heaven and earth attract each other and thus all creatures come into being. Through such attraction the sage influences men's hearts, and thus the world attains peace. From the attractions they exert we can learn the nature of all beings in heaven and on earth."[1]

At some point in our lives, most likely we have wondered whether we are the only ones in existence destined to be alone forever. If there is a perfect partner for us, a soulmate, where could that person be? Our questions, like all questions, arise from the answer, which is deep within. They do not originate from a superficial desire, but from our heart's yearning for shared experiences in life.

We have chosen to incarnate into a world where our connection with all other life is central to our spiritual growth. We arrange our significant relationships at a deep, interconnected level before we incarnate. We agree to meet other souls in order to resolve old issues, expand our awareness, explore the world, evolve and reconnect with Source. We consent to be willing to love and be loved unconditionally in order to be intimate with the world. Unconditional love lifts the mask of the world, showing us a hidden order, allowing us to witness and also to *be* magic.

Once our agreements, or meeting arrangements are in place, like a magnet attracting us toward our destiny, we are drawn toward our soulmates. In her captivating book *Sacred Contracts,* Caroline Myss suggests that this pull is more than destiny:

> Because life is so complex and there is so much to "see"—about ourselves, the world, and the Divine—we have Contracts with many people in our lives. . . . These are people you are not simply destined, but required to meet.[2]

She calls these people our Noble Friends.

We use the term soulmate when we think of a perfect romantic partner because we have no other term to express what we feel. But we do not necessarily fall in love with or marry our soulmates, although that frequently happens. Soulmates are those souls that have been with us through many lifetimes as our lover, mother, daughter, father, sister, son, partner, or adversary. With our soulmates we have played out all possible combinations creating and working through karma. Consequently, there are any number of individuals with whom we can fall in love and be happy, at least until we work through the reasons of why we are together. We could say that no matter who we are with at any given time, that person is the perfect soulmate for us because our level of awareness attracted us to each other. Our Noble Friends are different. As the other part of us, our agreement says that we are compelled to meet.

If the mystery of trying to figure out if you have agreements, or how these agreements might work, gets too overpowering, it is time to simply ponder this possibility. Suppose that just prior to incarnating, we are part of a whole entity—both male and female. When it comes time to embody, we split into either a male or female in order to experience the physical world from that point of view. This split creates our complement—or Noble Friend. As we get ready to go to our earthly destinations, we might have a conversation that goes something like this:

"I'll be the man and you'll be the woman," he says. "It will be wonderful. You will have skin that I can touch, lips I can kiss, a body I can hug . . . ," a thought wafts through his mind and he smiles. "We'll play and argue . . . "

"Argue? I don't want to argue."

He laughs. "Of course we'll argue. After all, we'll be human. To not disagree would deny our humanness. There'll be so much passion—high voltage energy—because we are from the same soul, we'll have to argue to resolve our perceived differences and come together. Underneath the disagreements are unconditional love and awareness—our soul knows we are trying to shake off the cobwebs, to unite. Besides, making up on Earth is so much fun, it's an electrified charge unlike any we know here."

He picks up his backpack full of memories, issues, talents, agreements, and baggage and starts toward a tunnel of dazzling white light.

"Do you have to go so soon?" She asks.

"Hmm. 'Fraid so. I see my mother is on her way to the hospital now."

"Wait! Where do I meet you . . . and when?"

"I don't know. You'll have to follow the clues."

"Clues?"

"Yes, the Universe gives us clues, signs to help us open to who we are, to our greater selves. As we get to know ourselves, and move toward wholeness, we'll be drawn to each other."

"But what if I don't recognize you?" she says tearfully.

"You won't," he replies with a grin. "This time, I'll recognize you. Besides, we are destined to meet."

It is 1988. I locked eyes with a new friend as he sat beside me on my sofa. Until that moment he was just a friend whose energy, conversation, and company I enjoyed. I barely knew him. Why only the night before I had realized how happy I was with my life—exactly the way it was. For an instant I had even wondered if a man would fit in. My heartbeat picked up. In the back of my mind something that felt far away tugged at my awareness, "I know him from somewhere, I simply can't think where."

A delicate gossamer veil that I had not noticed previously, hung between us. As if pulled up by unseen fingers, the veil slowly lifted, and I recognized Michael. Michael—my other half, the spiritual partner for whom I had left my previous life; the man who was destined to stand beside me, tap me on the shoulder when I needed it, and confront me with my own blindness. In another space and time we had agreed that he would be the person I depended on to see what I could not see myself.

Did I recognize him as my complement—my Noble Friend? Not until that moment. Did he recognize me? Yes, but he discounted what he felt. Nine months after our paths crossed at the Monroe Institute, Michael came to me for a private reading in Boston. He asked about his soulmate. "You've touched her hand," I said. "And I see an M."

"It's Winter," he thought, even though at the time he was dating a woman named Margaret. But every time he reflected on our conversation, he thought of me. He would reject these thoughts. "No, it can't be Winter. She's the teacher." He had other clues, including the psychic who started to physically describe me when he yelled, "Stop! I don't want to know any more."

I have serious reason to believe that our unseen connection was being revealed when we arranged a friendly ski trip with two other friends. Michael suddenly, with no obvious cause, developed a horrendous ache in his stomach, the emotional center, just as we were about to leave. He stayed behind that night, trying to sleep on his bedroom floor, but writhing in pain. It turned out that there was no physical reason for his distress—the only reason was that his entire life was about to change.

I also had clues, but I had to be hit over the head to see them. Before we met, Michael had come to me in my dream-state and kissed me. Another time, I had heard the words, "Waiting for Michael" when I awoke. And even though I had spent a week 24/7 as Michael's trainer, I totally blocked him from my awareness and could not remember him several months later when someone mentioned his name. You can imagine how my curiosity was aroused when my usual psychic abilities would not work. Hard as I tried, I could not bring up a visual picture of him. But even more significantly, there was a bigger clue—a fact. I simply enjoyed being in his energy. I felt contented and complete when we were together.

Dreams and messengers can play an important role in announcing our future partners, if we are open to the possibility that answers come in all sizes and shapes. In the story below, at first glance, it may appear that Jennifer and Robb were separately constructing their futures, but on closer inspection we see that their lives were inexplicably intertwined, in ways we may never understand.

Before reading the story of how they found each other, it is worth mentioning that years earlier, Jennifer's first love, Jason, drowned in a cold Maine lake. The date was April 17, 1992, the Good Friday before Easter. On that same day, several states away, Robb was on a hiking trip. An unexpected winter storm blew in, complete with low temperatures and snow, and her future love, Robb came close to death from exposure to cold, but he survived. Merely coincidence? It would be another five years before Jennifer and Robb would meet.

Robb

I guess you could say that I was depressed and ecstatic by turns. I had been running like that for quite a while: trading a straight head, moments of clarity and revelation, with the inevitable hangover. When I was nineteen this suited me quite well, but after three years I found my dreams and my writing full of the endings of things, apocalypses, and escapology. After five years, my thoughts all keyed on the assumption that I was a burnt-out mind, living in a destroyed shell, in a destroyed apartment piled high with junk and the remnants of a girlfriend who had moved out without leaving any indication as to why—except that she left on Independence Day.

At least I had my music. I played saxophone in my own group called Julia Galaxy with my two closest friends. Our music was a perfect reflection of all that I think we wanted to believe about ourselves: imperfect and rough, loud and brilliant, distressed and breaking up, but beautiful despite everything. We composed our music spontaneously and found ourselves deep inside of the right-here, right-now moment during our performances. It was inside that music, playing with eyes closed, that I first made a connection. I felt a swelling in my chest and a widening of the inside of my head and the notes became something automatic, producing melodic complexities that were the music of my dreams.

I woke up one Tuesday in March and felt a compulsion unlike any I had ever felt before to clean up everything in my life. I spent twelve hours a day for a week cleaning my apartment. I began the process of paying thousands of dollars in overdue bills. I got a telephone for the first time since it had been disconnected a year earlier. I washed my clothes every time I wore them. I quit smoking. Around that time, I saw Rob Brezny's horoscope for that month.[3] It said something along the lines of "Get ready. Something is coming and if you are not ready you will miss what could be the most important thing in your life." No mistaking the urgency in that message, so I doubled my efforts and found myself sitting in a perfectly clean apartment, legs crossed, listening to records with a wide-wide smile on my face by the end of March.

Jennifer

When I lived in Virginia, I started a new job at Time-Life. On my first day, a woman I had just met asked me if I was in a relationship. I said I was engaged and she said, "Oh. That is too bad, because I know your soulmate. He works here. His name is Robb Monn." I giggled nervously and shrugged it off.

Over the next year my relationship with my fiancé deteriorated. I realized that he was not the man I was meant to marry. At that time, I still had not met Robb.

Robb

I can remember Jennifer's first day at the company very clearly. We were walking in opposite directions down a long hall. I marveled at how beautiful she was; she has the most strikingly clear dark blue eyes and a serious face. She walked closer and I made what was a pretty serious goof: I became so intimidated by her that I didn't manage to say hello. She didn't either and marched by with a stern look. It would be a year before I spoke to her. I would see my future wife a thousand times before I would begin to get to know her. She often filled my thoughts, though—most often it would be an odd vision, her head slightly above mine so that her eyes looked down into mine.

Jennifer

One night I dreamed that I was stuck at the bottom of a pool and could not get to the surface. Suddenly, a young man I worked with, but hardly knew, Matthew, dove in and pulled me out of the pool. He pointed down a path and said, "You are supposed to be with us." I looked up and amongst a group of people there was a tall handsome man with beautiful blue eyes. He took my hand and we began walking down this new path.

Robb

My best friend, Matthew had a little crush on Jennifer, whose office was across from ours. He made up reasons to talk to her and would keep me posted on their conversations. I was shocked for two reasons. Matt was in a serious relationship with a woman he really cared for, and Jennifer sounded like she was different from what I pictured, she wasn't—well—mean, which was what I had assumed from her serious face.

Jennifer

The day after my dream, Matthew walked into my office for no real reason. He sat down, we began chatting and we talked for over two hours. By the end of our conversation, he had invited me to come with a group of other colleagues to see his band play.

Robb

And so it was a year later that I was sitting with my legs crossed in my perfectly clean apartment, penniless but not in danger of having anything repossessed, contented, but curious as to what would come next. My earlier depression spoke to me of another long slow decline as the best possible case, but I had hopes for something more. I was listening to a song by Bjork. It struck me as a wonderful miracle of a song, so I set the CD player to play it over and over: "I miss you, but I haven't met you yet . . ."

Jennifer

Three nights after that dream, I walked into the bar to watch Matt's band play, and sitting on the floor putting a saxophone together was the handsome man from my dream. He looked up and smiled and said, "Hi. I'm Robb Monn."

Robb

That Sunday my band played our weekly gig and Jennifer was there. I was still unable to speak to her, but I played for the first time with both my connected method—and a purpose. I played love to her and entered into a completely new kind of place while playing than I had before. I hoped that I was conveying my feelings and my soul.

Jennifer

I'll never forget the feeling when I first heard Robb play. It was like vibrant electricity mixed with a strange feeling of being invaded. Part of me never wanted him to stop playing and part of me, hand held over my heart, wanted to run out of the room.

I could feel him so strongly; it was beautiful and frightening. I had said no more then "hello" to the man, and yet it was as if we were instantly connected from our cores.

Robb

And then I asked her out on a real date. We went to my favorite restaurant, a taoist teahouse, and walked around Washington, DC, for six hours, visiting all my favorite bookshops and talking about everything. She took my hand that night and the rest of our lives began to unfold together.

Jennifer

Robb and I are now married. Matt was the best man at our wedding.

There is no rational explanation for how the stranger knew that Robb was Jennifer's soulmate, or for how Jennifer's dream coincided with her destiny as it unfolded. An underlying principle brought awareness of Jennifer's future husband to a stranger, and then brought him into Jennifer's dream state. This same principle, all part of a divine interrelated Universe, led her to intuitively know that she was engaged to the wrong man.

How do we know if we are meant to be with a partner or to be alone for this particular journey? In her beautiful book, *The Path of Prayer,* Sophie Burnham says that she once asked her spiritual director the troubling question, "How do I know the will of God? How do I know if this longing is really what the Universe wants of me?"

"Did it ever occur to you," her director replied in a thoughtful way, "that God puts desires in your heart, in order that you will execute them."[4]

Our desire for partnership is the divine within ourselves and the Universe wanting to unite with itself. This sacred marriage is alchemy. Alchemy is not about turning lead into gold, rather it is an allegory about the changes that take place in our body, mind, and soul when we align with our spiritual nature.[5] The alchemists' ritual of fire, burning off the dross, is meant to get beyond our ego—our stubborn, materialistic, and fearful ways—and find our spiritual center. The use of fire for this process suggests that it is a challenge.

It is not until these fires are burning that our transformation and our pull toward union with our other half, our complement, begin. Then we will be strong enough to see ourselves clearly reflected in the mirror of partnership. This by no means suggests that we are perfect, but rather that we have simply heard and answered the call of our own yearning for wholeness.

If you desire a relationship and it has not shown up, first ask the question, "Why do I want a partner? Do I expect my partner to fill a void in my life? Do I hate to be alone?" When we are insecure we fret and worry, resist change, and grasp and cling to others out of desperation. Our grasp is full of tension. It is psychically draining and the effort exhausts us and those we cling to. Anyone we are attracted to will feel our urgent energy and stay as far away as they can. And why shouldn't they? Our neediness will squeeze the life right out of them. If both of you are needy, then you will exhaust not only yourself, but also each other. You will, in time, have nothing left to give. Perhaps our most difficult earthly task is to unconditionally love ourselves. Only then can we unconditionally love another human being. Everything else we do is, in effect, preparation for this.

Finding our partner and entering into a relationship is not about filling a void. Relationship is about stretching—going beyond our limitations—becoming more than we ever dreamed we could be. Partnership requires that we be as whole within ourselves as possible, accepting the challenge of aligning our mind and our yearnings with our heart and knowing that we have left our ordinary life behind.

The effects of love, of having our heart aligned with our mind have been shown at the Princeton Engineering Anomalies Research Lab

(PEAR).[6] There, studies in consciousness-related physical phenomena have been under way since 1979. In these studies, they have measured the power of intention on a Random Event Generator (REG), a pinball machine, a water jet, and a little robot. Their results show that intention influences the machines at significant levels. Even more importantly, two people working in pairs produce stronger results than a single individual. On average, two people of the opposite sex have twice the effect of two people of the same sex; and two people in love have seven times the influence of a single individual. It is not just intent, but love that has the greatest effect on the machines. And if it can affect machines, just think what love can do for the world.

A hidden order does not promise that there will be no arguments or challenges when we meet our complement. In fact, they are a necessary part of our agreements to help each other stretch. A hidden order does not require us to marry or even kiss. It does, however, compel us to meet. What we do once we meet is our choice.

Experiential Practice

These experiential exercises open by asking you to turn to the Master Practice in chapter 11, Dreams. It has been my experience that dreams are innately tied to our physical world. I met my husband, Michael, in a dream and Jennifer Monn saw herself walking away with her future husband, Robb, in a dream. At times when I have been doing a private reading for someone I have noticed that they have no dreams, no vision of what they want. We must dream as if our life depends upon it. It does.

Next I ask you to journal your thoughts about love. It is my feeling that most of us really do not know what love is. We confuse it with need, sex, security, and not being lonely. Sort out your thoughts about love—even if all you have to say is, "I don't know what love is."

Look around to see if you really have room for your partner.

When I moved in with Michael he owned a virtually empty house. It was as if he was waiting for me to come along and fill it with my dishes, my clothes, and my furniture.

The invocation and ritual will help you draw love into your life.

Getting Started

Begin with the Master Practice, Dreams, in chapter 11. Then continue with the exercises below.

Daybook

Write down all your thoughts about love. Remember to allow your ideas to flow and keep your pen or pencil on the paper while you write. No editing. Don't stop to decide whether you think something is accurate, or worth including. If it occurs to you, write it down—write down what you hear.

Answer the following questions: What do you believe about love? What do you believe to be true about relationship? What simple pleasures bring you joy? Now, write a love letter to yourself, cherishing your unique characteristics. Next, write a love letter to your partner, lover and/or perfect complement, relishing their ability to bring you joy. Write the letter in the present tense, as if they are in your life now.

In Susannah Seton's *365 Simple Pleasures*, she suggests keeping a bedside journal in which you only write love-notes to each other. "There's nothing like getting into bed, feeling that little lump under your head, and realizing that you have sweet words from your beloved to read before going to sleep."[7]

Tool Bag

If you are creating a relationship, it is important to make space for your partner. Remember Robb's story? Starting with your bedroom, remove any clutter. Is half of your bed filled with books, papers, or clothes waiting to be laundered or hung up? Clear off the bed and definitely open up the area under your bed. Can you walk to your bed unimpeded? Is there subtle, negative energy caused by a former relationship, argument, or illness in your bedroom? If so, take a cup of sea-saltwater and walk around the room, sprinkling the water as you say, "I purify this space. All negative energies are banished. I open to love."

The bathroom is next. Is there room for the toiletries of a second person? Make space. Buy a second toothbrush and toothpaste in anticipation of the arrival of your partner. Continue to make space for your complement in all areas of your life.

Food for Thought

> Love does not consist in gazing at each other but in looking together in the same direction.
>
> —Antoine de Saint-Exupery

Observe your thoughts. Any time you think, "All men are a certain way," or "All women are just alike," you are off-center, repelling the partner that you wish to attract. What you think you see is a projection—what you think, you become.

Invocation

In the Celtic tradition there is a belief that if you send out goodness from yourself, or if you share that which is happy or good within you, it will all come back to you multiplied ten thousand times. The more love you give away, the more you will have.

This Celtic Friendship Blessing is for all of you, that you may find your *anam cara*, your soul friend.

> May you be blessed with good friends.
> May you learn to be a good friend to yourself.
> May you be able to journey to that place in your soul where there is great love, warmth, feeling, and forgiveness.
> May this change you.
> May it transfigure that which is negative, distant, or cold in you.
> May you be brought in to the real passion, kinship, and affinity of belonging.

May you treasure your friends.
May you be good to them and may you be there for them.
May they bring you all the blessings, challenges, truth, and light that you need for your journey.
May you never be isolated.
May you always be in the gentle nest of belonging with your anam cara.[8]

Ritual

Dreaming can be a way of creating, planning, and moving your dreams into reality. Dreaming can also be a way of discovering the hidden order flowing through your life.

You will need:

- A rose-colored candle
- An herbal mixture (see directions below)

Prior to your bath, mix 1 cup dried rose petals, 1 cup dried rosemary, ½ cup dried lemon verbena, and ½ cup thyme together and store in an airtight container. According to your taste, place ¼–½ cup of this mix in a muslin square, then tie it shut or place it in a large tea ball. Place the herbal container in a quart of boiling water and let it steep for twenty minutes.

Draw your bath and pour in the herbal infusion.

Soak in the rose-scented water and visualize being a beautiful, sexually appealing, confident person enjoying a loving, mutually satisfying relationship as you inhale in the fragrance and energies of the rose. Repeat every Friday (Fridays are ruled by Venus) for a month.

After taking your warm, herbal bath, spray your pillow with lavender or place a small lavender-scented pillow close to your head, where you can roll onto it. The scent will help you remember your dreams. Slip between clean sheets. Before you fall asleep, place your hand over your heart. Center. Ask to meet your partner in the dreamtime and to remember the encounter when you awaken.

6
Life and Death: Before the End

Only when we are no longer afraid do we begin to live.

—Dorothy Thompson

Although I was always interested in the idea of the supernatural, I was not aware of just how interested I was until my freshman year in college when my father died. His spirit showed up in the middle of the night to tell me he had just had a heart attack and was no longer among the living. He wanted to give me a few details on how to handle his funeral and, I might add, the rest of my life. I got out of bed, packed and repacked my bag, decided my running clothes were not appropriate for a funeral, and waited. As I waited for the call informing me of his death, I was acutely aware that my greatest fear—daddy would die and leave me—had happened. Did this fear stem from knowledge of an agreement the two of us made before we incarnated—that we would be together for only a few years this time around?

From the moment of his death, 12:23 AM, my father's presence stayed with me, comforted me, planned his funeral, and gave me guidance. The night after his funeral, I was sleeping in the bed with my mother, when he came to the foot of the bed and asked that I join him at the top of our stairs. I did. He hung over the stairs in front of me and we talked. I could not see him, but I could hear him and feel his closeness. He told me about an insurance policy that he had recently taken out—so recently the insurance agency said it was not signed. They were mistaken, it was signed and it paid for my college education.

In our society we fear death because we do not know who we are. We think we are simply flesh and bone, and are vulnerable. But our true nature is that of Spirit and Spirit is not vulnerable. My father's death showed me, through direct experience, that our soul is immortal. It survives this body. Life is continuous. I think this continuity shows itself in many different forms and in many different dimensions (dreams, déjà vu, the feeling that you've known a stranger in some other place and time.) The *I Ching,* which reveals our position in the general scheme of things, says that certain areas in our lives and in nature are fated.[1] This is not an easy concept for Westerners to accept. If this is true, an acceptance that certain things are destined would be very empowering in both our personal and worldly affairs. We would not spend our precious energies on the impossible, but we would perceive what is truly possible. Our aims and desires would be in harmony with the needs and flow of the cosmos—with the cosmic order. However, although the *I Ching* suggests that our destiny may be already written in the stars, it also clearly says that in a period of advanced culture, it is important that we achieve something significant—that we stand apart in order to benefit the whole.

I picked the stories in this chapter because they seem to suggest an ultimate plan, a cosmic order lying beneath our lives—a plan that protects us from harm or brings about what would appear to be an untimely death.

Robert

> Looking back, it is obvious that there was a path. Life may have seemed aimless to me, that I was wandering in a chaos of choices, but I have also been lucky—there were always hints, signposts, a knowing that I was on the right path even though for a long time I had no idea where that path might lead.

One such knowing was at the beginning of the Second World War, when the Germans invaded Holland, in early May of 1940. The world as it had been crumpled and died. Germany had prepared for years, and France for almost as many years, but Holland and Belgium had not. It took five days to complete the occupation of Holland. Belgium had fallen even more quickly.

On the fifth day the Germans bombed Rotterdam. During the previous four days our lives had been severely shaken. Telephones and electricity worked only sporadically, but we still had water. Stores were empty or barricaded. Cars did not run because gas stations were closed. I was in Rotterdam visiting some of my parents' friends who lived on the outskirts of the city. I could not leave. When German planes flew over in waves, dropping bombs and incendiary devices on downtown Rotterdam we stood precariously on a narrow ledge on their roof, speechless.

In the middle of this, the telephone rang. It had not worked for days, but there it was. It was definitely the telephone and it was ringing. Closest to the door, I ran down to answer it. Not quite believing that there would be anyone at the other end, I said, "Yes . . .?"

Even more surprising, the call was for me.

A crackling voice said, "There is a boat in Amsterdam that is bound for New York. If you can somehow get to Amsterdam in the next six hours or so, you can get on. You are on a waiting list for passage to New York, are you not?" The message came through in bits and pieces, and was repeated several times.

I could hear other voices in the background, but the caller, growing more and more insistent, kept repeating, "Make your way to Amsterdam. There is a place for you on that boat." I could leave the madness of Holland for the promised land—New York, America . . .

Without thinking, I said, "No, I am not leaving."

I hung up and sat down. What had I done? I heard the drone of planes dropping thousands of bombs on the city only a few kilometers away. I desperately wanted to get away from Holland, from Europe, from the madness I knew to be all around me. I wanted to go to America. Holland had been cold and miserable, friendless, the few months I had been there. America? I knew nothing about America, except of course that it was the land where gold lay on the streets, and beggars became millionaires.

Six months earlier I had called my father in Indonesia. He had agreed to subsidize my studies in America as he was doing in Holland but I had to make my own arrangements to get there. Now as I watched the bombs fall on Rotterdam, I was being offered passage on a boat that would go to New York.

And I had said, "No."

As if a window had opened somewhere in my brain, I knew clearly and absolutely that I would survive this war, because there was something I had to do after it was over. Throughout the war, I never lost this knowing.

Two days later I heard that German planes had sunk the boat as soon as it reached the English Channel.

The Germans captured me three times. The first time was when they began picking up Jews. The usual practice was to call on Jewish households at two or three in the morning. The people were then marched to a central collection point. From there they were shipped first to a camp in Holland, then to concentration camps in Germany and Poland.

I would get up very early in the morning and walk alongside these sad, bedraggled people, recording their messages in my little notebook: "Tell my aunt," one would say, giving me an address, "There is something we want her to have under the flower pot in the dining room," or "Let my brother know that our daughter is safe." Most messages were innocent, perhaps not very important, but it made the people feel better.

One day I was not paying attention. A German staff car drove by, stopped, picked me up, and dumped me through a door at the headquarters of the Gestapo.

Sixty or more people were already there, standing around, silent and scared. Even though I did not appear on any Jewish Registers, I knew that I would be processed along with everyone else. I also knew I could not scale the ten-foot-high brick wall surrounding us. There was only one way out—through the Gestapo headquarters building.

Without thought I walked inside. German officers were everywhere. It took no time at all for one to grab me by the arm and yell—German officers never talked, they yelled—"What the hell are you doing here?"

A sentence popped into my head. I had no preconceived plans of what I would do once I was in the building. I replied in German, "I just came in the front door and presented myself to the front desk. I'm looking for my friend Lieutenant Hanson. The guard at the desk told me to come back here."

My captor dragged me to the front desk where, fortunately, the guard had just changed. A new man was settling in. "This man says that someone here told him to look in the back for Lieutenant Hanson . . ." Before he could say more, someone nearby said, "Lieutenant Hanson just went on vacation. He left last night!"

My captor released my arm.

"Thank you," I said. I walked out the front door.

Later in the war, I was caught a second time. It was dangerous to travel at all, so I chose to travel around five or six in the evening when it was getting dark, and the trains were full. My train arrived in Utrecht, Holland, about the same time as trains coming from four other directions. Before we came to a full stop the loudspeakers blared, "The German High Command orders all passengers to disembark and proceed to the station square."

It was dark but I could see that we were surrounded by machine gun posts along the periphery of the square in front of the station. My first thought was of Lidice, a small Polish town where the Germans had massacred the entire population as punishment for killing German officers. Nobody said a word. It was eerily quiet. The fear was palpable.

Again, I knew I had to get out of there as soon as possible. I looked more closely at the machine gun posts all around. Some were letting people out slowly, after checking their papers. Not only were my papers not good enough for a careful inspection, I was carrying a gun and papers for the resistance in my briefcase. A quick glance told me that one of the machine gun posts had only one man. All the others had two men, one manning the machine gun, the other checking papers.

I moved to the one man at the end. When I was still two spaces behind the person he was checking, I purposefully bumped into the man in front of me. He dropped his papers and bent over. I stepped around, quickly flashed my papers to the German soldier, and walked away.

It took him a second to realize what I had done. But then he yelled out, swiveled his machine gun and began shooting. I walked calmly to one of the narrow streets that led away from the station. I did not run, zigzag, or try to dodge the bullets. Turning the corner, I sagged against the building and wet my pants.

My last close encounter occurred between the cars of a train. Germans were checking papers. The officer stopped and asked me for my papers. I locked eyes with him, all the while thinking, "You cannot touch me." After a minute or so, with a grunt of disgust, he lowered his eyes and moved on.

It was more than twenty years after the end of the war when I understood my reason for surviving. I met the most primitive people remaining on earth, untamed Aboriginals. From them I learned how to find my most inner self again.

I learned that there are moments of such clarity of experience that we see that we are no longer separate beings; moments when we are in such a blessed space that we flow, without ego, without selves, without time. These are moments when we are the harmony and we cannot experience anything because we are inside what is. It is then that we are not our own creation. We stumble upon these moments; in fact, we have to learn to let them happen, allow ourselves to be swallowed.

Vance

In January of 1992 I read the following intriguing story in Maine's *Portland Press Herald.* I was familiar with sea smoke and how it could blanket the coast of Maine, rendering visibility to near zero.[2] It wasn't hard to imagine 40-mile-an-hour winds, a wind chill of -54 degrees, ice, and darkness and conclude that this was no ordinary tale. The story simmered in my mind for years, eventually giving rise to the idea of *The Hidden Order.*

Vance Bunker will tell you that this really isn't his story. That's partially true. Rudy Musetti's wife, Marilyn DiBonaventuro, gave me his name. Vance and his wife Sari were kind enough to help me with the details. This story is about the 75-foot tug, *Harkness,* Captain Rudy Musetti, his mate Arthur Stevens and Arthur's daughter Robyn, and Rudy's buddy Duane Cleaves who went on the trip for fun.

It is about Rockland Coast Guard Petty Officer Ronald Chadwick who had to make a quick decision between taking to the rescue his 44-foot cutter—designed to weather the rough seas, but adding considerable time to the trip—or taking the 41-foot boat which was twice as fast but less maneuverable in rough water, which could possibly put his own men at risk.

This story is about the islanders on Matinicus and Vinalhaven who monitored the *Harkness*' status and reported to the lobster boat,

Jan-Ellen, and about the people all along the Maine coast who huddled by their scanners, praying the *Harkness* and their rescuers to safety.

It is about the two men who braved the elements aboard the *Jan-Ellen* with Vance, Paul Murray, and Rick Kohls.

It is a story about those who live on the islands of Maine, and Maine lobstermen. As Vance told me, "Rescues happen frequently, they just don't get as much publicity. Fishermen have done this for centuries, without acclaim, without notice, without expectation of reward."

But even more, this is a reminder to all of us about a way of being in the world. When someone calls for help we don't question *if* we will help, but rather, *how*.

Vance's Story

January 16, 1992. Matinicus Island, Maine. (Twenty miles out to sea, Matinicus is the outermost inhabited island on the eastern seaboard.) A thick sea smoke had settled in over the water, completely enveloping the coastline. Winds were howling at forty miles an hour. Thermometers registered four below on land. Some would say this was a wild night, weatherwise. To a Maine Islander, this was just typical January weather. The lobstermen on Matinicus had stayed off the water that day because of the "vapor." They were waiting for the cold weather to break.

It was about 6:00 PM. Rick Kohls (my sternman) and his wife were over for lasagna when we heard the *Harkness* radio the Coast Guard over the scanner, "*Mayday*. . .we're going down." I radioed the *Harkness* to see what kind of trouble it was in. "Two feet of water over the stern," they reported.

It didn't take long for us to realize that there were few people on the island, and the Coast Guard would need all the help they could get. I called Paul Murray, the island's mechanical wizard, and asked him to come along—just in case something went wrong with my boat, the *Jan-Ellen.* Paul had been with me on the water before; I was used to him.

It was 6:40 when we headed out. Visibility was zero—I couldn't see the bow of my boat. In all my life on the sea I had never seen saltwater ice coat the windshield so quickly, or freeze so hard on the deck. We couldn't hurry because if I opened the throttle the spray would rush onto the boat and freeze. The ice would make the boat useless.

The captain of the *Harkness* told us he was north of the island—he could make out a green flashing buoy. The problem was that there were two buoys out there, separated by a mile and a half. We headed toward Northeast Point. Because I couldn't see, I watched the compass as Paul and Rick stood behind me, calling out the Loran fixes.

Just as we cleared the harbor (at 7:03) transmissions from the *Harkness* ceased. We knew then that the tug had gone down and we were now probably searching for bodies.

From the time we lost the conversation, I don't remember anything. I felt sick. My stomach just knotted up.

It took us fifteen minutes to reach the Matinicus buoy but something was wrong. Our position didn't match the position the *Harkness* had last given us. The Coast Guard gave me a new set of coordinates—near the ledges of No Man's Land and Zephyr Rock, 1.5 miles northeast of Matinicus.

When we got close to the Zephyr buoy, I saw lights that belonged to the Coast Guard's 41-footer. This is where all of us thought the *Harkness* had gone down. We looked over the side, but most of the time we couldn't see each other, let alone somebody in the water.

We knew there wasn't much chance they would still be alive, but Rick and Paul kept looking over the sides. We slowly scanned the water, the cutter behind us, everybody looking, fearful of running over a body.

Suddenly, Rick looked *up* instead of down. A beam of light pierced the sea smoke just at the moment Rick Kohls glanced away from the water and into the sky.

"I couldn't believe my eyes," Rick said. "I saw a light shining straight up into the sky above the sea smoke."

It wasn't much of a light, but its impact was dramatic. Unable to see, I followed Rick's directions until we cruised directly to three men hooked together, frozen to a wooden extension ladder that had come loose from the wreckage of the *Harkness*.

A small, three-cell battery flashlight was frozen to the glove of Duane Cleaves. I don't think he was aware that he still had it, because his hands were too cold to hold onto anything. When we pulled him in he couldn't walk or move. He was close to being a dead man. All three were half dead.

The ordinary three-cell, garden-variety flashlight had been a Christmas present to Arthur Stevens from his daughter Robyn. She purchased it because her grandmother had said, "Flashlights are always useful. You just never know when you might need one." Robyn thought Arthur would really like this one because it was waterproof and he spent a lot of time on the water.

Harkness captain Rudy Musetti said that when he finally abandoned ship he was certain that the rescuers would not find him in time. "You can't survive more than a few minutes in that water, and I was already on the verge of hypothermia." When the *Harkness* crew was pulled from the water, the combination of wind and temperature created a wind-chill factor of fifty-five degrees below zero.

"I'm not real religious," Rick said later. "But something happened that night."

A series of random events—yet invisibly connected—had to occur in order for the crew of the *Jan-Ellen* to rescue the *Harkness* crew. Somehow a wooden ladder freed itself from the *Harkness* and floated up to them at night, in 40-mile-an-hour winds, rough seas, and sea smoke, and they were able to grab hold of it.

Stevens' daughter picked a little flashlight for his Christmas present and that flashlight made its way to the mitten of Duane Cleaves. What are the chances that the beam of a flashlight that's frozen onto the glove of a drowning man would point straight up into the sky? It should have been submerged. But the beam did point straight up and Rick Kohls just happened to look up in time to see it. And what if Rick had hung over the *other* side of the boat instead?

One other life-saving event took place prior to the rescue. After a few minutes in the water, Arthur Stevens knew that he was dying. He didn't care, he was so cold that he couldn't think straight. He let go of the ladder because it made no sense to hold on any more. Soon after, Rudy slipped under the water, but resurfaced choking. "The sound felt like *someone* had slapped my face," Arthur said. He kicked back to the ladder, hooked himself around Rudy and held his captain's head out of the water.

If any *one* of these events had not taken place, the *Harkness* would have joined the long list of ships lost around the ledges of Matinicus Island.[3]

Carol Muske-Dukes

On August 13, 1981 I was in Florence, on my way to Umbria, where I would spend the weekend visiting a poet friend. She had arranged for me to ride down with a friend of her brother's—an actor. I waited in the lobby of the hotel where we had arranged to meet. I looked up to see a tall, dark-haired man who said, "Sorry I'm late. By the way, I'm David Dukes," as he approached.

I understood, as I took his hand and gazed into those blue eyes, how we know when our lives are changing before us, how we sense something—a little ripple in time, a kind of swerving from the present into the imagined future. I knew he was going to happen to me—it felt, suddenly, like what the Italians call *destino.*

But I really didn't believe in fate—that something beyond our power could determine our lives.

Nineteen years after we met—October 9, 2000—I stood with our seventeen-year-old daughter, Annie, on the front steps of our home in Los Angeles waving to David, who was flying back to the set of a miniseries called *Rose Red*, shooting in Seattle. He had been home for the weekend. I was sorry to see him leave, but was cheered thinking he'd be home in a few days for a three-week break. I was pleased, too, because I'd just finished making changes to the copyedited manuscript of my new novel, *Life After Death.* David had asked to take a copy with him to read on the plane, then decided to wait until he got back to read it. I was eager to have his opinion of this final version of my unconventional novel about life and death, about (among other things) a woman whose husband dies of a heart attack on a tennis court.

A few hours later, around 7:00 that night, the phone rang. The young man at the other end of the line identified himself as a tennis pro at a recreation center in Spanaway, Washington. This was where my husband went after his afternoon flight—for an early evening tennis workout. And this is where he dropped dead of a heart attack on the tennis court.

What we do when we write remains a mystery. The imagination is a force, a guidance system, an ungovernable power. I think back to 1981, to Florence—the moonlight pouring over us, how we shook hands. What seemed so much like fate, I believe, was my sudden intuitive knowledge of David—and a sense of where that knowledge would take me.[4]

The Titanic

Is the imagination of the writer a conduit for a hidden order? In 1898 Morgan Robertson published a novel that told the story of the demise of the supposedly unsinkable ocean liner—the SS *Titan*—and seemed to foretell the sinking of the *Titanic*. Robertson's story featured a similar name and a long list of imagined events that later coincided with the *Titanic's* sinking.

Like the *Titanic*, the *Titan* left on her maiden voyage from Southhampton, hit an iceberg and sank. Almost a mirror-image of the White Star Line's *Titanic*, the *Titan* displaced 70,000 tons, measured 800 feet, and transported 3,000 passengers. The *Titanic* displaced 66,000 tons, was 882.5 feet in length, and carried 2,207 passengers. Both ships were driven by three propellers.

At the time Morgan Robertson wrote about the *Titan*, the technology to build such a ship did not exist. It was simply his imagination. In Robertson's novel, the arrogant owners of the *Titan* were so convinced of its unsinkability they provided only twenty-four lifeboats for the 2,500 passengers. The *Titanic* carried only twenty lifeboats, half the number required. Over 1,500 passengers lost their lives when it sank.

There were many who did not make the fatal trip on the *Titanic* because they had dreams or premonitions of a disaster. One person who ignored his own precognitions was journalist William Thomas Stead. In 1892, twenty years before the event, he wrote a story in which he described in detail the horrifying sinking of a great ocean liner. Despite this, he disregarded his own warnings and sailed on the *Titanic*. He was one of its victims.

The 2000 Presidential Election

While some authors simply let their imagination flow, bringing with it information from a hidden blueprint, others use tools, such as astrology, to tap into the unseen. Astrologer/freelance writer Jim Shawvan speculated in October 2000 that the results of the 2000 election would be delayed. In April of 2001 he followed up with an uncanny specificity about George W. Bush and the Presidency.

> Although we can never know in advance the exact events that will unfold under a given set of astrological indicators, it is quite possible to be clear about their nature. I set out to look for dates when the planet Mars, in President Bush's astrological chart, will be activated. I am concerned about the dangers that such activation brings. The potential for violence always exists.

Shawvan went on to say that our president has a pattern of planets that grabbed his attention, including ones that show deception and confusion, like Mercury and Neptune, because they reinforce

> the probability of trouble with one or more foreign governments . . . which would certainly be characteristic of a terrorist conflict such as the one involving Osama Bin Laden.
>
> Although we cannot say whether these indicators point to terrorist attacks, an attempted assassination, or a more conventional war, they do seem likely to bring at least one major violent event affecting the U.S. and its president; and perhaps start an entire new scenario of violence, which could last for quite a while.[5]

Four months after Shawvan's article appeared in *The Mountain Astrologer*, terrorists struck the World Trade Center and the Pentagon September 11, 2001. If we, or our intelligence agencies, had read and believed his article, would things be different? Could I be telling the stories that follow?

Robert Redford

On September 10, 2001, Robert Redford had a business meeting in New York City that ended early enough for him to catch a flight back to San Francisco. Otherwise, he would have taken the same flight he frequently took when he stayed over, United Flight 93—Newark to

San Francisco. Flight 93 was the flight on which passengers fought back against the hijackers. It crashed in Pennsylvania.

"I would have been on that flight if I had not finished my business," he said flatly. "For some of us, it's 'There but for the grace of God . . .' I fall into that category."[6]

Lucy

April 13, 1990. While attending Airborne School in Fort Benning, Georgia, I fell and ripped everything out of my ankle except my Achilles tendon. After surgery, I was forced to stay home for several months while my ankle healed.

I was the only one in my office not deployed to the Gulf War. This made me the very visible, current intelligence briefer for the four star general of a major command. This accident changed my career path and put me in the position I hold today.

Now fast forward to September of 2001. August 23, I fell off my flat shoe and broke my fibula above my reconstructed ankle. I returned to full working days on September 10. I was still on crutches.

It was one of those mornings. I had so much to do and no time to do it all. My husband was traveling. It was up to me to take Jack, my son, to preschool and then get to an early meeting. I picked up my mug of coffee and briefcase and called to Jack to hurry up . . . I had an important meeting at 8:30. Of course my precocious seven-year-old had more important things on his mind. He was standing at our front window watching the last remaining trees in his favorite playground be demolished by a bulldozer for a new subdivision that was going in across the street.

"Mom, you have to watch this big equipment," he said.

"No. I've got an early meeting, we've got to hurry."

Jack, always responsible, always polite says, "Please Mommy, can't we watch the big equipment from the front porch?"

I never give in. Jack never asks twice because I never change my mind. But on this morning I put down my briefcase. For the next ten minutes we sat on the front stoop and watched a large cement culvert being lowered into the ground.

"We really have to go now, hon. I'm late for my meeting."

When I dropped Jack off he was different from other days —he was clingy. This was significant. At age seven it is not cool to hold onto your mother.

The traffic on the way in to the city was worse than usual, but I refused to listen to the radio. I popped in a Tony Robbins tape and mentally geared myself up to excel in my meeting.

There was an open parking space close to the building, and I headed up the walk. I would only be twenty-five minutes late if I rushed. A woman caught up with me. She kept trying to carry one of my bags. Being strongly independent, even on crutches, I refused her assistance. "I'm late for a meeting. Do you mind if I just move on?"

"I used to be in the army," she said. "I want to get back in. Can you help me?"

At first I said no, but she was insistent, actually slowing me down because she kept talking and holding on to my arm. When we reached the front door to the Pentagon I said, "Give me your name and telephone number and I'll pass it on to someone who can help you."

Pulling out a used metro ticket, the woman wrote down her name and number and handed it to me. By now I was really late for my meeting, but instead of heading there, I went by my office. What difference would five more minutes make?

A television set was on. "What do you mean the World Trade Center was hit by aircraft?" I asked. And then I felt it . . .

"What just shook the building . . . ?"

It was September 11, 2001. My meeting was in the wing of the Pentagon that was struck by a hijacked plane.

A couple of days later I pulled out the metro ticket and dialed the number. I wanted to thank the woman for detaining me. The number she had written down did not exist.

The World Trade Center

On the 106th floor of 1 World Trade Center, Adam White was at his Cantor Fitzgerald desk by 7:30. He had told his mother in suburban Baltimore that he would be in the office all week before leaving that Friday for business in Rio.[7]

An older firefighter came in to the emergency room on a stretcher, wearing the uniform of a unit from Jersey City. He was in cardiac arrest from the smoke and debris he had inhaled—he was 64, retired, and had a bad heart—he was not supposed to be there. His family was unaware that he had put on his uniform again and gone out with his old crew. He died on the day that hundreds of firefighters died.[8]

Rescuers searched diligently for survivors in the World Trade Centers debris with no luck, yet a member of a search dog team was found alive after being buried for four days.

Why? Why did some live, so many die? Did those who died September 11, 2001 at some higher, deeper level of consciousness *choose* to die a mass death? Was this our collective unconscious speaking, trying to give us a message? If the World Trade Center disaster had not happened, would our world be different?

Margaret Clarion

There are many who have been attempting to right inequality and injustice for years. Margaret is one of these people.[9] Did her soul choose to be born to political activists, to tread a path for justice, to grow up in a country of terrorism and political assassinations?

> When I was six years old my father was killed because he was a political activist. I have always thought that it is my legacy to speak up against injustice, but that by speaking up I would probably be killed. I often wonder if my days are numbered.

In the late '80s and early '90s I worked for the Red Cross supplying food to the nomad refugees in Africa. One day David, the pilot who was in charge of provisions, asked me to be his companion for the trip. Refugees on the ground never knew if an airplane was coming to aid them or to kill them. It was not unusual for them to shoot at planes. And of course, the opposing soldiers did not want food brought in to the refugees so they would fire at planes. In spite of my misgivings, I agreed to make the trip.

I remember that David tried to ease my mind as he loaded the plane. "I've been doing this journey forever. I know what you're afraid of, but the refugees need food. Nothing bad will happen to us. When we let fear stop us from doing what needs to be done, our enemies have won."

About an hour into the flight a bullet passed through my side of the plane and hit David in the head, killing him instantly. I never learned who fired at us. He could have been killed by the people we were bringing supplies to, who did not know we were there to help or by the soldiers who were against us.

In times of emergency we often discover a power within us we draw on. I had never flown a plane, but when David fell back in the seat, I got in front of him and landed in the field where the refugees were waiting.

Over the next two years I continued my work with the refugees. There were two groups of soldiers we had to work with. One group was honest and helped us get the food to those who needed it. But another group stole the food and sold it on the black market. It never reached the people it was intended for. I got tired of this. I finally reported what they were doing to the authorities.

It was not long after I went to the authorities that I woke up one morning feeling very troubled. My uneasiness continued as I dressed and prepared to go feed the refugees. When I got to the

> food tent there was a strange tension among my co-workers, all female. The energy, something, was not right.
>
> I saw a friend at the door of the tent. "You don't look well," I said.
>
> "I left home feeling fine, but now I have this funny headache," she replied.
>
> I walked around the tent thinking, I've got to get out of here. I could feel something wrong. I later learned the soldiers had come the evening before because they mistakenly thought we slept in the food tent.
>
> There were fifteen of us there that evening. Although the uneasiness was so thick you could cut it with a knife, we went ahead and dished out food. It was dark when we got ready to leave. That's when the soldiers came, from out of nowhere. I can't say that I knew the soldiers were coming, but I knew something was wrong.
>
> The soldiers took us outside, lined us up against a wall, and shot us. All of my friends were killed. I was only hit in the ankle.
>
> When the soldiers learned that I did not die, they went to my home looking for me. I had been there, but I left an hour before they arrived. They beat my mother and burned my home and all my personal papers. Friends smuggled me out of the country.

Margaret believes that providing education to our third world nations is needed in order to bring peace to the world. Does the life she lives today answer the question of why the bullet passed by her head? Why she was not killed like the rest of her colleagues? Is there a harmony—a hidden order—that connects her life with the needs of the Universe?

The stories I have told here hardly establish a hidden, cosmic order as fact. However, they do suggest that an idea that has been around for thousands of years—that certain things are fated—cannot be lightly dismissed. In the least, it is something to question.

Whether we believe that our death is written in a cosmic plan, or will happen in a random moment, there is one thing of which I am certain. We do not have time to indulge ourselves with petty grudges, judgments, or remorse. Stories such as these remind us to live fully—to let each of our acts make a difference. In that way, our last act—whenever it may come—will embrace the very best of who we are.

Experiential Practice

At this point you are familiar with turning to the Master Practices at the end of the book. Because without our breath we would not be alive, we return to chapter 10, Following the Breath—Quieting the Mind. This exercise will help bring you to a centered space within which you will know that nothing is ever lost or forgotten and there is no place to go. Everything is here, now, in the present moment.

Getting Started

Read and perform the Master Practice exercise Following the Breath—Quieting the Mind in chapter 10. It is from this centered space that you fulfill the following exercises.

Daybook

My grandmother felt that the dead were always close, that they did not live far away. Because of many of my own experiences, I share her view—the eternal dimension is here, now. Kahlil Gibran said as much in *The Prophet:*

> You were born together, and together you shall be forevermore,
> You shall be together when the white wings of death scatter your days.
> Ay, you shall be together even in the silent memory of God.[10]

I believe that when someone dies a portal opens, giving us a glimpse of those dimensions, what some would call the eternal world. You can talk to those no longer living, but often putting your thoughts on paper can be more powerful. It is as if we really mean what we say and we are willing to write it down.Write a letter to someone no longer living. If you have regrets about something you did not do before they died, tell them. If you are still holding on to resentment, forgive them. Tell them you love them. Write as if they are looking over your shoulder reading every line.

Tool Bag

Live today as if it were your last day on earth. Let each act be purposeful. Call people you have not spoken with for a long time, tell people you love them, be fully present with life and with nature.

Food for Thought

> Neither the sun nor death can be looked at steadily.
>
> —La Rochefoucauld

Ritual

Although sorrow and grief are part of life, there are times when we are in the midst of these states that we feel the need to do something to lift our spirits. Oranges, by their refreshing aroma, can help you release sorrow, even if only temporarily.

Make an infusion by covering the zest of one orange with boiling water and letting it steep for a while. Then pour the infusion into your bath, or simply put slivers of orange or orange rind into your bathwater.

Invocation

Although I can't prove it, I believe that expanded consciousness, whether it be through relaxation, some altered state, or in our dream state, takes place in a another "space"—a dimension altogether different from this reality. This "space" is a place that has realities as complex and valid as our own. Both personally and with clients, my goal is to get into that space, which musically could be called the "space between the notes."

Begin by thinking of someone who has died and who you would like to make contact with. Find a quiet place where you will not be disturbed. Sit or lie in a comfortable position, close your eyes, and notice your breathing. Just be aware of your breath as it moves in and out . . . in and out.

After a few moments, slowly inhale through your nose and imagine that your breath is being drawn down into your lower abdomen. Your lower abdomen should fill out naturally when you do this.

Gently exhale.

Breathe in again, all the way down into the core of your body, two inches below the navel, and two inches in. The Chinese call this the *tan t'ien*, the place in your body where your life force or chi resides.

Invite the spirit, or person you wish to contact, to join you.

Imagine there is a warm, white light that is moving down from the Universe into the top of your head . . . then slowly moving on down through your body. Release your mind from any tension, any worries, and let any thoughts that come up simply drift by like a cloud floating across the sky.

Inhale deeply. Bring the light up the sides of your body and down again. Allow the light to flow into all areas of your body.

When the white light reaches the soles of your feet, bring it up the back of your legs, your spine, your neck, up over your head. Let it spill forward over the front of your body until finally you have circled your entire body in a cocoon of white light.

Allow the images of the person who you wish to contact to float into your mind. If you like, you can imagine that they are sitting in their favorite chair and you are there with them.

Ask the image anything you wish. You can do this telepathically with a thought, or a feeling of a thought. Some questions you might ask are: Who is there with them? Do they ever visit living individuals in their dreams or thoughts? Do they have any unfinished business? Is there anything you can do for them? What will be their next incarnation? From their perspective, what do you need to know at this point in your life?

When you feel complete with your visit, thank them for their time and bring your awareness back to floating.

Begin to float back, toward your physical body.

Feel the energy moving down through your body and feel the warmth of your heart center.

Tell yourself that you will remember all you have seen and experienced. And that you will return rested, yet energized.

And when you are ready slowly return to full waking consciousness.

7
Manifesting: Creative Power

> There is an energy—a vitality—a life force that is translated through you into action. Because there is only one of you in all of time, this force is unique and will never be repeated. If you do not use it, the world will not have it. It will be lost forever.
>
> —Martha Graham

My interest in the powers of the mind simmered for years before I took action. I read about how consciousness worked. I borrowed my experiences from others. This was how I had been taught—open the head and pour in the information. But fresh out of college, I could feel something was not right. Living was uncomfortable and difficult. Once I was gainfully employed, I had quickly discovered that being obligated to the same duties every day felt like nothing more than prison, except in prison you can watch TV. I exhausted hours wondering who made up the rule that we had to spend the best part of our lives working five days a week. Why not work three days, or only Saturday and Sunday? Why work at all? I decided that Joseph Campbell was right when he said, "Work begins when you don't like what you are doing."[1]

An Episcopal cathedral was not far from where I lived, and late one night I found myself slipping into a back pew to barter with God to help me. I was a pro at trading off with the Source when I wanted to abdicate responsibility for my life. Those days I was willing to give Her whatever she asked for.[2]

I really didn't know what I wanted, just that I did not want what I had. "Help" came one rainy Saturday afternoon while I was browsing through a bookstore. I accidentally knocked over a display of *Psycho-Cybernetics* by plastic surgeon Maxwell Maltz.[3] "God flashed," to use Belleruth Naparstek's expression, and a hidden order revealed itself. While restacking sixty books, I took the opportunity to look inside.

Although Maltz was mainly concerned with self-image, there was another significant ingredient in his writing that was appealing. He wrote about what he called the Law of Attraction. Simply put, it says that what we think about we attract into our lives. If we affirm or pray from lack we give energy to that lack even if we are affirming abundance; but if we come from a place of optimism, anything is possible. He asks readers to make a list of what they want, picture what they would like to be and have, and believe that it will happen.

Maltz's philosophy is supported by many ancient traditions. The Buddha said, "We are what we think. All that we are arises with our thoughts. With our thoughts, we make the world. What we think we become." The Upanishads of ancient India observe that "when the mind rests steady and pure, then whatever you desire, those desires are fulfilled"; books of the Han Dynasty tell us, "Nothing is impossible to a willing mind"; Lao Tzu believed that people and their attitudes and actions are inseparable from the physical phenomena surrounding them;[4] and, in fact, the first tenet of psychology is that we get what we reinforce.

Within an hour of crashing into the books, I sat in the middle of my bed making my list. Solely on trust, I followed this up by writing three letters: one resigning my present position, and two requesting graduate school applications. Six months later, with a work-study fellowship in hand, I was back in school. The following month I met the man I described on my list—my first husband—complete with blue blazer and khaki pants.

It appeared that once I focused on what I wanted, all kinds of synchronistic events, meetings, and material assistance happened, supporting the direction I wanted to go. My desires were being met.

This was my ego (that part of me that identified with my physical body and its senses and *thought* that it was separate from its surroundings) separating itself from real wisdom. If left unchecked, it would ambitiously take credit for my creative thoughts and manifestations—it would claim that "I" did this.

But there is another way of looking at it. The creative power of a hidden order permeates the Universe. It is primal, Light-giving, active, strong, and of the Spirit. The *I Ching* says that the "creative alters and shapes us until we attain our true, specific nature, then it keeps us in conformity with the Great Harmony [a Hidden Order]."[5] It is more likely that the events on my list manifested because they were part of my path—a hidden order was shaping me.

Most indigenous tribes understand these dynamics. In *Mad Bear: Spirit, Healing, and the Sacred in the Life of a Native American Medicine Man,* Doug Boyd tells of sharing a meal with Mad Bear:

> "I thought to myself," Doug said, "Mad Bear simply said 'dig in.' This man does not say 'grace' nor, in fact anything but 'dig in.' Reading my thoughts he responded, "We don't ask 'give us this day,' though I have no disrespect for those who do, we don't ask anything of the Great Spirit, but we think of ourselves as being here to do what the Great Spirit asks of us.'"[6]

It would seem that we are confronted with a paradox. On the one hand, as we evolve and seek to know our spiritual nature; as we listen to our intuition, observe our dreams, and stay open to synchronistic events occurring in our lives, we come to realize that our yearnings are not separate from those of a hidden order. Our desires originate within a divine force beyond our skin-encapsulated ego and are there to help us align with our path.

On the other hand, the mind-body connection we discussed earlier in chapter 4, and the Law of Attraction imply that not only are we in some way responsible, moment to moment, for our own health and well-being, but we are also accountable for everything in our reality. Our health, career, relationships, and environment all present us with opportunities to observe what we are creating from the dramatic to the mundane. This has huge ramifications and can reveal unexpected ways to solve the ills of the world.

How do we reconcile these two, apparently different views of how things manifest? Do we create our world in the present moment or before we reincarnate? Is everything in our life preplanned or do we have a choice in what we draw into our lives?

A hidden order is full of seeming contradictions. Because we have lost touch with our greater selves, we feel helpless to change our lives. But in a higher, more expanded state of consciousness, there are no inconsistencies because it is all the same. Our biggest challenge is to stand undisturbed by the apparent paradox and allow this great mystery to unfold and guide us moment by moment.

Thinking about a Universe where reality is shaped through our thoughts may be easier for the Buddha and some quantum physicists, than it is for the rest of us. Yet when we read Malcolm's story that follows, can we draw any other conclusion?

Malcolm

In October of 1991, I was living in the quiet community of Oakland Hills, California. One beautiful Sunday morning I had settled down to watching a football game when my wife called to me, "Malcolm, come outside and look at the sky!" When I went out I was shocked to see that black smoke covered over half of the horizon.

I hopped on my bike and peddled up the hill to take a closer look. Across eight lanes of freeway Berkeley was ablaze—a massive fire was raging out of control.

On numerous occasions I had thought about what it means to be detached. More than once I had asked myself, "Do I have any possessions that I consider really precious?" There was only one—a custom electric bass.

> When we were told to evacuate, I still had ample time to pack my cherished possessions. I slowly walked through our house thinking, "I'm prepared for a big change—if that's what this is." In that moment I made a commitment to the Universe, that I was going to believe that everything was happening exactly as it was supposed to be.
>
> We took our cat, our two cars, and a change of clothes. Nothing else.
>
> At the end of the driveway, before filing off with our neighbors, I stopped and mentally placed a bubble around our home. Then I drove away.
>
> We watched the evening news from my sister-in-law's house. Our neighborhood was engulfed in flames. The next morning, despite the fact that the entire area was cordoned off, we snuck through the lines and hiked to our house. When we reached our street, my wife did not recognize it. The entire area looked like a war zone—it had been reduced to rubble—a chimney farm at best.
>
> Incredibly, in the middle of the devastation, our home was still standing, though everything within a hundred-yard radius of it had burnt to the ground. On all four sides of our home the fire burned up to the fence and stopped. A perfect square around the house was untouched. The fence was not charred and the grass was still green. The only damage to the building was one cracked window.

When we join with creative energy, I believe we can influence what manifests. At some level, perhaps unconscious, Malcolm felt this connection and used his focused intent to protect his home. He said he was ready for change, ready to let go of everything—he had no attachments to the material world. He walked his talk by taking nothing with him but the cat, a change of clothes, and his car. But he did stop and place a bubble around the house. Did the bubble he placed over the house protect it? Was it saved because of the design of a hidden blueprint? Or, was it merely a coincidence that his home was the only one that did not burn?

The Universe attends to our needs constantly, answering our silent, often simple requests. For example, my husband Michael frequently asks the questions, “Why the disparity among individuals? At what point does ‘enough’ for one person, become ‘hoarding’ for another?”

One unusual incident happened when we went to a movie. Michael wanted candy. He filled a small bag with chocolate then stood at the counter to pay for it. But before the candy was weighed, he discovered he had no more money. He raced outside to the car, scooped up all of the loose change in the console and ran back inside. The candy was weighed, and he had exactly the amount of money he needed. For the next three days, both of us had similar incidents take place. Exactly what we needed, when we needed it, manifested.

What we ask for does not always arrive in the package that we expect. If we insist on controlling how or in what form our desires will materialize, we place limits on what can manifest. If we make our request, then relax and stay open to whatever comes, we find results far greater than anything we could have imagined previously.

My friend David was working on his master’s degree in anthropology while he maintained a full-time career. What he asked for, he got, but not in the manner he expected. Now he is very careful about how he asks for what he wants.

David

> It was a time when I really wanted to talk to someone about my ideas. I wanted to meet a person who would understand. My work was as an undercover agent and there wasn’t anyone I

> dared open up to. My daily mantra was, "Just send me someone I can talk to."
>
> One morning I got up and a hippie was sitting on our front steps. "Great. A drug addict wanting a free handout," I thought. I'm a narc, I can smell a druggie a mile away.
>
> "I'm a friend of your daughter," he said in broken English. All the while I am thinking, "Outstanding. Now my daughter is running around with a drug addict. Just leave before I have you arrested." But I didn't say these things. I grumbled that I would wake my daughter.
>
> As luck would have it, my daughter had plans and I ended up giving this guy a ride to the bus station. You guessed it. He was not a drug addict. He was from Russia and had been traveling the world, which explained his disheveled appearance. He had a scholarship to an Ivy League university—in anthropology. He wasn't what I expected, but he was exactly what I wanted.
>
> About the same time I desperately wanted to leave undercover work. My studies were far more fascinating. Besides, I was tired of the cops and robbers game. Retirement was too far away for me to practically consider, yet I kept thinking about not being a cop anymore. One night, after a high speed chase through the city, I caught and pinned the guy down. He begged me to be easy on him. I relaxed my grip and he kicked me solidly in the shoulder with his heavy boot. My shoulder was smashed. I am no longer in law enforcement, but this wasn't the way I intended to leave. The disability package doesn't make up for my constant pain. You know the cliché, "Be careful what you ask for."

The act of manifesting may simply be the way a hidden order brings us together with those we have agreed to meet, or rediscover. Julie carried a question on her heart for twenty-three years. The surprising answer came in its own time, on its own schedule.

Julie

Seven years ago my mother, sister, and I were having breakfast at the Waldorf Astoria on our vacation in New York. The topic of southern breakfasts came up, and we soon realized that the couple seated next to us was also talking about breakfasts in the South.

"You must be from the South!" My mother said.

"We're from Perry, Georgia," they replied.

"We're from Jessup, Georgia."

The man said, "This is so weird. We've been looking for a girl from Jessup for twenty-three years. She lived with us one summer and we lost track of her. She was such a big part of our lives."

"What was her name?"

"Julie Bennett," he replied.

Our mouths must have hung open for a full minute. I was Julie Bennett and I had been trying to locate this man and his family all these years.

When I was nineteen years old, I had been a swim coach on Sea Island, an exclusive, private island. This man and his wife had let me live for free in their maids' quarters in exchange for taking care of their three children. I loved those kids. At the end of the summer I reluctantly left for Hattiesburg, Mississippi, to finish my last two years of school. I lost touch with them.

The fall after I left Sea Island, all three kids and their father were in a serious plane crash. They all survived, but soon afterward, their mother committed suicide. The family moved to Perry.

Our constant thinking is always creating a momentum. But what and how quickly we create this momentum is directly related to our alignment with universal energy, creative intelligence, or a hidden order. Without an awareness that our experiences are a result of our thoughts, we persistently create the same life with very little difference, over and over again, year after year.

Mass Consciousness Manifestations

We cannot talk about manifestation without considering that, at some level beyond the physical, we are all connected, even though we experience things as if we are separate from everyone else. Our thoughts and the events of our private lives contribute to world events, and every night our dream life cannot be separated from the dreams of others. Jung called this connection between our individual self and humanity in general the collective unconscious. Human history suggests that our collective unconscious decided that intellectual knowledge—logical analysis—was more important than intuitive wisdom. The problem with this is that when we believe that we know everything or that we can find out everything if we intellectually diagnose and analyze events, it leaves no room, or incentive, to discover what we do not know. How does our mind affect our reality? Collectively enamored with the intellect, we seem to move further and further from the Truth. Our combined minds separate from real wisdom.

But our world is neither static nor absolute. Nature invariably prevails. Nothing stays the same; everything changes. Every action has its complementary reaction. When we swing too far in any one direction, the momentum will pull us in the opposite direction. Intuition is meant to be an equal partner with logic. Our pull toward balancing intuition with the intellect started gradually, but recently the pace has quickened. There is the sense that consciousness is attempting to stabilize the extremes in the world, not cause them. The *I Ching* calls this the time Before Completion:

> The conditions are difficult. The task is great and full of responsibility. It is nothing less than that of leading the world out of

> confusion back to order. But this is a task that promises success, because there is a goal that can unite the forces now tending in different directions.[7]

Our collective ability to affect change is supported by numerous studies that have documented the fact that our thoughts can and do influence others in profound and measurable ways. In addition to over 180 studies that have substantiated the positive effect of prayer on everything from other humans to yeast cells,[8] the International Peace Project in the Middle East found that when a critical mass, or one percent of the population, came together around the world to practice Transcendental Meditation, there was a measurable decrease in the number of violent crimes, suicides, terrorist attacks, and international conflicts worldwide.[9]

An international collaboration of researchers known as the Global Consciousness Project (GCP) is studying such extraordinary qualities of consciousness. Director Roger Nelson recently commented on the data they recorded on September 11, 2001 and the surrounding period. The evidence supports a developing global consciousness that reacts to events that have deep meaning.

> When we ask why the disaster in New York and Washington and Pennsylvania should appear to be responsible for a strong signal in our worldwide network of instruments . . . there is no obvious answer. This network . . . conceived as a metaphoric EEG for the planet, responded as if it were measuring reactions on a planetary scale. We do not know if there is such a thing as a global consciousness, but if there is, it was moved by the events of September 11, 2001. Maybe we became, briefly, a global consciousness.[10]

These studies reinforce ancient texts that say we can set our intention on a specific outcome and have it happen. Knowing this to be true, it is exciting to think about possibilities—individually and collectively. With this awareness we are compelled to focus our intention on creating a harmonious world.

To understand the creative power of manifesting, be open to what Spirit asks of you, the vision of the creative force, and the path of a hidden order. By aligning with that vision, you can create the future by adding energy to the image. If you can do this, everything else is inconsequential.

Experiential Practice

Your entire life is a reflection of what you have created. How you picture your future actually shapes it. Just as you have spent time learning to follow your breath, now is the time to focus on intent. Intention is our connection to Spirit, to our blueprint. We could say that intent is getting clear on what it is that you wish to manifest.

Lao Tzu credited most of the world's ills to the fact that people do not feel powerful and independent.[11] They fall victim to the desires of others. Without a sense of personal power, they are resentful and fear the unknown because they feel separate and alienated from anything that is beyond themselves.

The same holds true today, twenty-six centuries later. For the most part, as a species we have separated and alienated ourselves from nature, and from others who look, think, or pray differently. Unconsciously, we have disconnected from our own greatness. We do not feel powerful or in control of our lives. If only we realized that whatever we think about—good, bad, or indifferent—will be ours, we could change our lives and we could transform the world. A hidden order has huge plans for us if we can let go of our limiting illusions and believe in something greater.

Getting Started

Read and perform the Master Practice, Intention, in chapter 12. Then continue on with the exercises below, which will help you understand how to utilize intention in your life.

Daybook

It is important to be thankful for what we have, to express gratitude. How often do we stop to say, "Gee, I am really thankful that you are in my life," or "I am so thankful for my health, my home, my animals, my friends." We find it easy to ask for things, but often forget to say, "I am thankful." I believe that before we begin to create something new, it is important to take a moment to appreciate what we have already created—things we want to keep, and those things that we want to let go of.

As your new manifestations come into being, remember to say, "Thank you."

Begin your process of manifesting by quieting your mind and following your breath as you learned in chapter 10. As you inhale say, "I am an integral part of a hidden order." Relax, become centered, and get in touch with your creative, powerful, inner self. Now set the stage for future manifestations.

- Write a thank-you note to the Universe expressing gratitude for who you are and everything in your life, even things that challenge you.
- Decide what you want to create. This is the hard part. Most of us don't know what we want.
    - List ten things in your life that you want to keep, all the while maintaining awareness that all things change and nothing is forever. For example, I want to keep Michael, our animals, our good health, our home, our good friends.
    - List ten things that you want to let go of, things that no longer

serve you. For instance, let go of a victim or poverty mentality.
  - List thirteen things you want to manifest. If it helps you can divide your list into categories: spiritual, relationship, career, environment, travel, and so on.
- Write out your five-year goals as if you have already achieved them. For example: We now own our home and we are debt free. Be sure that your goals are what you want, not what someone else thinks you should want.

Tool Bag

Make room for your manifestations. What have you been holding on to that no longer serves you—old clothes, wounded relationships, beliefs? Give the clothes away to someone who can use them; surround the wounded relationships with white light and wish them well; write down all of your beliefs that prevent you from living the life you would like to live. Burn it. Make a list of five risks you would like to take and make plans for checking them off.

Food for Thought

> If you want the whole thing, the gods will give it to you. But you must be ready for it.
>
> —Joseph Campbell

Invocation

What we create in our lives, our personal well-being, is a reflection of our connection with others. Read the following aloud three times to strengthen your intention to connect to the other people in your life.

> May I be medicine for those who are sick, a partner for those who are lonely, a bridge for those who need to cross over, and a light for those who are blind.
>
> —A prayer of the Bodhisattva

The Silent Seven Rules of Manifesting

All life is energy in form. Every physical object, every situation, every event that has ever taken place started as an idea. When we focus our energy into the direction we want to go, it will gradually manifest in physical form, taking shape in the world. Consider that any work of art, any dance performed, any object or invention, began with a thought. The big question is, where did the thought originate?

Rule One: Intend. Intention is more than simply thinking about creating. Intent takes place at a much deeper emotional level.

Rule Two: Ask for help. There are many ways we can ask for help, and we do so all the time. How many times have you pleaded, "Help me," to God, the Goddess, Spirit, or the Universe when you needed a hand? We have many quiet helpers, just waiting for us to ask. I frequently ask "the spooks," my unseen helpers, for help finding something I have lost, opening a jar, or just making things easier. Reach down inside of yourself and draw on whatever you believe is good and true, and make your request. Be clear. Ask that you be in touch, and in alignment with the creative force. That in itself is enough.

Rule Three: Believe. Even if you are not sure manifestation works, act as if it does. For one minute, one hour, one day—suspend your doubt, your disbelief. We make up our lives all of the time. This is creativity. Think of things you have manifested in the past, your successes. Remember that you are an integral part of a hidden order. You have all of the energy and help of the Universe available.

Rule Four: Cause no harm. This is the Rule of Three: What you send out comes back to you. Ill will returns threefold.

Rule Five: Focus. You must have absolute and complete focus on what you are creating. The target you want to create is already in existence now, in actual or potential form. Focus on the end result that you want, not how to get there. Set your manifestation in the Now—the eternal present—not in the future. Do not lose patience. It will appear in its time.

Rule Six: Stay detached. Don't be attached to the details of how things will manifest. There is a Buddhist saying that we plant the seeds and the grass grows on its own. We don't go out every day and pull on the grass.

Rule Seven: Never, ever, tell what you are manifesting. Keep silent and hold it close to your heart. Remember that as children we were advised to "blow out the candles" and not tell our wish. Keeping our manifestations to ourselves not only keeps the energy from dissipating, it adds to it.

In addition to the rules, there are two ways of being. First, strive to always express appreciation for what you receive—say "Thank you." And second, give unconditionally. Do not give in anticipation of receiving, but give from an overflowing sense of abundance because you are in touch with a source that is continuously renewed.

Using Props

Sometimes we need a little more than just our imagery or visualization to help us clarify what we want to manifest. In these instances, the use of a physical prop or aid can be a very powerful, useful technique in manifesting. The objects or symbols help us focus our mind and energy on our end result. This exercise will help you discover which props work best for you.

Magic Box

Create a magic box that is exclusively for your manifestations. Describe what you want to manifest in written, pictorial, or symbolic form and place it in the box. When you close the lid, say, "This, or something better, now manifests for me, in perfectly satisfying and harmonious ways, for the highest good of all. So be it." Leave it there. This is a wonderful way of letting go of what you are creating. After two or three months, open the box and see what has been manifested. Give thanks for it. (It may be more than what you imagined.)

Treasure Map

Make a map for what you wish to manifest in one single area of your life. You can have several separate maps. Draw, paint, or make a collage from magazines, cards, books, photographs. Be sure to put yourself in the picture. Last, and most important, use a symbol or word that acknowledges that you are aligning with universal Source from which everything comes. Write the affirmation of highest good on the back of the map: "This, or something better, now manifests for me, in perfectly satisfying and harmonious ways, for the highest good of all. So be it." Place the treasure map where you can see it.

Ritual

You will now learn several different rituals which you can use at different times depending on the quality you would like to strengthen in your life. These rituals are best performed in a quiet orderly room or preferably, outside in a natural setting, because clutter draws old energies to you. Bathe and dress in comfortable clothes. Take your telephone off the hook. If you like, light a candle and burn incense. Make certain that you are alone and will not be disturbed. If you have pets, allow them in the room with you if they will remain calm.

To Gain Clarity

All information is available to us in the present moment. When we are not distracted, we are clear. Don't rush forward in your mind. Stay present. Sense "what is" in the now.

To begin this ritual, mix ten drops of lavender oil with ten drops of lemon oil in a glass cup or bowl. Massage a few drops on your temples. Say out loud, "I see, hear, and think clearly. The veil of fog lifts from my senses." After using these oils, neurotransmitters in your brain will trigger the production of biochemical secretions, which will, in turn, affect your mood, feelings, and emotions.

Often the reason we are not clear on a subject is either (a) we don't know what the question is or what we really want, or (b) we don't like any of the answers we seem to be receiving. I believe the best way to get clarity is to first refine the question we are asking. To do this, take a deep breath. Imagine that you draw white light into your body, with the intention that you are shedding light upon the area in which you desire clarity. Be open to the Universe, trusting that you will receive divine guidance for your highest good. If any negative thoughts arise, accept them, thank them, and send them off in a little burst of light. Then simply let it be. Go for a walk. Listen to a piece of music. Observe nature. If you happen to be at a lake or pond that is still, with no ripples, you can use it as your reflecting pool. Watch the clouds float across the sky, or simply look at leaves, stones, or sticks as they fall naturally. Your answer may not come immediately, but it will come in its own time.

Prosperity

Prosperity, like everything else, is experienced in our mind. If you believe that money is evil, non-spiritual, you will block its flow to you. Have you placed limitations on yourself surrounding the issue of money? Years ago when I started practicing the art of manifestation, I decided that I wanted to see the balance in my checkbook at one thousand dollars. It was not long before I reached my goal. Unfortunately, I did not think further. For five years my balance remained the same, no matter what I did, until I realized I was manifesting exactly what I said I wanted.

Money is in our lives to assist us with our life purpose. Before you undertake this ritual, ask yourself what do you really need? What is the use of acquiring what you do not need? Somewhere in between our yearnings and our letting go in death, we must find a balance—

how much is enough? We must find the balance between what assists and serves us, and what distracts us from living life.

Creating Prosperity

For the following ritual, select a Thursday, Wednesday, or Sunday, on a waxing moon—when the moon is changing from new, or black, back to full. You will need:

- A bayberry candle taper
- Cinnamon oil or plain olive oil
- A saucer
- A coin from funds you have won, a windfall profit, or that someone has given to you unexpectedly

Purify the candle by rubbing the oil on it from center to top, and from center to bottom, visualizing your desire while saying, "I manifest abundance, prosperity, wealth, and success."

Place the coin in the saucer and fasten the candle onto the coin with a bit of melted wax. Light the candle and gaze into the flame, imagining money swirling around and cascading down the side of the candle with the melting wax.

Allow the candle to burn down a little every day for as long as you can supervise it. When the candle has completely burned down, remove the coin and carry it in your wallet. When you receive your funds, pass the coin on to another in need.

Creating Peace

In *Global Brain,* Peter Russell says that "The image we hold of the future plays a role in helping that future to emerge."[12] Peace starts within each of us once we know what peace feels like. If it is peace of mind that we seek, we must look at our own beliefs and expectations and be prepared to change them. They may be wrong.

Lie still, not moving. Follow your breath in and out. Allow yourself to feel your emotions, your body, the mattress or floor. Continue to follow your breath and imagine a white light flowing into the top of your head, down through your body. Allow the light to flow through and around you, then outward in all directions, into the world—into the Universe. Visualize those who seem to be promoting the opposite of peace, wrap them in white light. See everyone and everything wrapped in white light.

Resolving a Difficult Situation

Sit quietly, mind your breath and bring the difficult situation into your mind's eye. Notice how it feels emotionally. In your mind's eye, create a silver platter and imagine the situation resting on the platter. Offer the platter up to the Universe with the message, "I am unable to resolve this situation. Please assist in its resolution. Thank you." There is nothing more you need to do.

Using Imagery

This ritual can be used for anything you wish to manifest. I have incorporated several elements of manifesting here. You can use all of them at a time, or only one—whatever feels right to you.

Clap three times

This calls your spiritual helpers. Clap five times to increase the flow of universal energy coming into your body; clap five more times to increase the amount of universal energy coming into your body even more.

Create a clear mental image of the object or situation you wish to manifest. Make sure you put yourself in the picture. See it as already existing, present tense, and put as many details in the picture as you can. If you do not visualize, intend what you want to create and focus on how it feels to have it.

Mentally place your picture in a pink balloon—pink is the color of love and harmony—and take it to a favorite spot and release it. Watch it float off above the trees, into the clouds, and beyond. As you release it say, "This, or something better, now manifests for me in perfectly satisfying and harmonious ways, for the highest good of all."

There will be times when you will wonder if you are actually creating your life, or are just wonderfully in harmony with what the Universe is sending your way. Then you may realize that it doesn't make any difference.

If your manifestation isn't working, it may not be in alignment with your true purpose; or perhaps you have been requesting the wrong thing. We ask for our purpose in life, but we don't want to have to change; we ask for our perfect mate, instead of asking to be the man or woman our mate will be drawn to; we ask for fortune and fame when what we really want is unconditional love. Ask Spirit if you are asking for the right thing. Request that your path, and its purpose, be revealed to you in a dream, guidance from a friend, in a book, or a song. Ask for help.

8
A Shared Consciousness

> I believe in God, only I spell it Nature.
>
> —Frank Lloyd Wright

During the late 1960s Dr. James Lovelock, in looking for evidence of life on Mars, looked at the Earth from the viewpoint of an extra-terrestrial and wondered why the Earth was different from its closest neighbors, Mars and Venus. He concluded that our planet appeared to be a living being in its own right—a self-evolving and self-regulating living system. Because the ancient Greeks called their Earth goddess Ge or Gaia, embodying the idea of a Mother Earth, Lovelock called his hypothesis Gaia.

We do not have to look far to find evidence that life in our biosphere Gaia is supported by an unseen order. The ability to self-regulate the salt content of seawater is just one example. Seawater is about 3.4 percent salt by weight, and has probably been under 4 percent for as far back as we have data, in spite of the fact that salt is continually washed in by the rivers. If it ever rises to over 6 percent, all life in the sea except for some bacteria would come to an end. If we had to run scientific trials in order to determine the perfect salt/water ratio needed to maintain life in our seas, one trial would take at least sixty million years. It seems Gaia got it right the first time.

But there is even more astonishing evidence of an underlying order to our Universe. Since ancient Greece, mathematicians, philosophers, scientists, artists, and theologians have pondered the mysterious relationship between numbers and the nature of reality. At the heart of this mystery is the number 1.6180339887—*Phi.*[1] Phi is fascinating because plants, animals, and humans all possess dimensional properties that precisely follow the ratio of Phi to 1.[2] An omnipresent number, Phi is considered to be divine.

Female bees always outnumber the drones, the male bees, in a hive. If you divide the number of female bees by the number of male bees in any beehive in the world, you always get the same number—Phi. Sunflower seeds grow in opposing spirals. The ratio of each rotation's diameter to the next is Phi. The petal arrangements of roses; mollusk shells; the breeding habits of rabbits; the shapes of the galaxies containing billions of stars; the distance from the tip of your head to the floor divided by the distance from your belly button to the floor; your shoulder to your fingertips divided by your elbow to fingertips; finger joints, toes, spinal divisions—all equal 1.618—Phi.

We are an integral part of Gaia, certainly in the physical sense—not only as seen by our Phi dimensions, but we have the same percentage of salt in our blood as our seas, and we need the by-product of photosynthesis, oxygen, for the air we breathe. But maybe we are integral in an even greater sense. What if we share the same mind, the same consciousness? What if the weather does not affect me, but rather I affect the weather?[3]

I grew up thinking I could influence the weather. On days that I wanted to go swimming I made certain that neither I, nor my swimming companions, would kill an ant. For some unknown, mysterious reason, killing ants made it rain. Of course, the fact that it did or did not rain may have had nothing to do with the survival of ants, but more with our strong desire for a beautiful day. Growing up in the mountains of North Carolina, summer was too short to allow rainy days.

Rolling Thunder, the Native American medicine man, was named because of his ability to call the rain. I don't think he based his practice on saving ants, although author Doug Boyd told me that he witnessed Rolling Thunder agitate a stinkbug immediately before the thunder, lightning, and rain rolled in. Doug guesses that because a stinkbug emits a small electrical charge when provoked, this electrical charge was the final piece Rolling Thunder needed to complete his rainmaking.

A few years ago I was in the Florida Keys, swimming with two dolphins, Annessa and Aleta, in a controlled environment. At the end of the swim they gave me a long pull to the far side of the lagoon, much to the dismay of their trainer, who kept blowing his whistle, requesting that they return to his side. Finally deciding to answer the whistle, the two dolphins tipped their rostrums, their massive gray bodies descended beneath the water, and they headed in. As my hands slipped from their dorsal fins, I thought, "I'm so far out here, why don't they give me a ride back?" Before I had completed the thought, Annessa presented her dorsal to me, a sign that she would pull me back to the dock. I like to think that in that moment we were of the same mind, sharing consciousness. If I do not take ownership of the thought that I wanted a ride back, but rather look at it as information that was conveyed to Annessa and me at the same time, it expands the possibilities of how I might interact more fully with my environment.

The following day an experience with a dolphin named Natua gave me another memorable experience of an expanded state of consciousness. During a training exercise, in front of several trainers and twenty students, my role was to ask three dolphins Natua, Delphi and Kibby a question that could be answered with a simple "yes" or "no" by the nod of their heads. They would respond to my hand signal. I asked my question and gave them the signal to nod their heads "yes." Kibby and Delphi responded to my signal. Natua just stared at me, not moving.

"What's wrong, Natua?"

A telepathic burst of knowledge, a picture language so dense that each image contained a thousand ideas, instantly appeared in my mind. I had given the wrong hand signal for the question I asked. My question and answer did not make sense, and in that moment I experienced why my question and signal did not go together.

If I get caught in the idea of what I think happened, the real truth gets lost. The tendency would be to anthropomorphize, to say that Natua told me how I messed up in a nanosecond. But it is preferable that I not think at all—but remain open—not try to figure out how it worked. I felt the information. Whether it came from Natua, the twenty people who were watching, Spirit, or our shared consciousness is not important. I have learned to be comfortable not knowing.

In many ways my experience with Natua was similar to the expanded state of consciousness that I get into when I am doing a medical reading—there is no separation between me and the person I am reading. In this state I could not tell you where "Winter" stops and the client begins because our energy has merged. It is not that I go somewhere to retrieve information, but rather I drop my boundaries and *become* the information—the Akashic Records, the Cherokee Temple of Understanding, the Universal Mind, the Philosopher's Stone. This state of shared consciousness could be the basis for understanding intuition, voices from the dead, psychic events, or the spontaneous memory of a past life.

Why is it that our ability to sense this shared consciousness seems to be heightened when we are in nature—hiking, swimming, sailing, watching a bird, or just being? Perhaps it is because we have left distractions and multitasking at home and we are able to focus solely on our environment, without thinking about anything else. Within any moment we can merge with our breath, become fully present, and on occasion simultaneously enter a state of interconnectedness, where we transcend our physical body and experience ourselves as being *one* with the Universe. In this state we recognize a deeper understanding of the nature of our reality, what I call a hidden order or blueprint. In this expanded state of consciousness we see meaning in all events. Everything is as it should be.

My first experience of this expansive state of oneness occurred outside on a cold, wet, rainy day in upstate New York. I was attending a workshop with twenty-four other people. Our instructions were to imagine that we were a tree and run universal energy from the ground up through our body. Freezing, I conveniently tucked the directions aside and planned my escape to warmth. I had already convinced myself that while some people might believe this was a valuable exercise, I didn't.

Just as I started to defect I noticed the soles of my feet were not simply warm, they were hot. Within moments the heat moved up my legs and a golden glow appeared in front of me. The heat moved to my knees, I got hotter, the glow grew brighter. Very quickly, other members of the group were becoming invisible. All I could see was this very bright, golden light. No longer cold, the intensity of the light and the heat in my body were reaching a critical point where I thought I was going to pass out. At that moment the teacher said, "Now bend down to the ground and run the energy back to the source from which it came."

Dropping my head, I bent down and my eyes fell on a blade of grass that seemed to be magnified exponentially. In that blade of grass, I saw the entire Universe; the intricate weaving of its fiber and variance in color was intensified by the water droplets on its surface. That instant I experienced being one with everything in the cosmos—I was the bright light, the heat, the blade of grass, the water droplet. I touched my head to the ground, and returned to my normal way of seeing.

It would be hard to think about nature without thinking about tumultuous weather—hurricanes, tornados, or blizzards. Storms have always fascinated me, possibly because I was born during the eye of a hurricane. I have noticed that my link with the world of Spirit seems to be more prevalent and clear during violent storms. Maybe it is the negative ions and ozone that open up the lines of communication, or simply sheer fear, but during these situations spirits and guides often reassured and calmed me, letting me know that all was well.

Possibly this is what the survival instinct really means. We have to reconnect with nature in order to hear and receive guidance more clearly. It is easy to dismiss our connection to a hidden order or blueprint when it shows up as an image or a thought; a felt sense such as heat, cold, or tingling in the body; or an emotion such as fear, depression, or anxiety that appears for no apparent reason. If you are trained in psychology, or work in the field of mental health, hearing a voice that is not attached to a physical body can have several meanings, among them: a stress reaction, a hallucination, or other psychological disorder.

Even though I taught abnormal psychology for years, and took every class in mental health law I could find—insanity defense, mental disability, competence, commitment evaluations, and involuntary treatment, to name a few—when I first heard a voice speak to me, I never once thought I was nuts. The very audible voice simply made a clear statement, telling me what was, with no judgment attached. Caveat: not all voices are necessarily helpful. Remember that if that voice comes from someone, for example, who has died, just because they are dead, doesn't mean that what they say is beneficial.[4] The following stories are told by friends of mine who are psychologists or former mental health clinicians. Fortunately for all of them, they went beyond their academic training, and listened to the voices they heard.

Kathy and Chuck Hall

My husband Chuck and I left Falmouth, England, late in the sailing season. Our plan was to hit a favorable weather window, head south to the Canaries, then to the Caribbean, making our way back to our home on the east coast of the United States. Violent weather quickly changed our plans and sailing down the English Channel took much longer than anticipated. Still ahead of us was the infamous Bay of Biscay which is treacherous, rough, and inhospitable most of the time. Our current weather would only make it worse.

While crossing the bay, both our CPT automatic wheel steering and our monitor wind vane steering unit broke, forcing us to hand steer in high winds and heavy seas for several days. After weathering our first gale we were exhausted. Rather than head into the next squall, we decided to heave to, stop the boat, and ride out the strong winds and sloppy seas below deck rather than put out a sea anchor.

We went below, closed the companionway, finally getting relief from the relentless sound of the wind, and had a hot meal without spilling it. Conceivably the single most threatening situation to voyaging sailors on the high seas is collision with a larger vessel. Chuck watched the radar to make sure we were safe from ship traffic. Later, I tried to stand a watch at the radar but I couldn't stay awake. We decided to leave the radar on while we slept. This is a common practice for single-handed sailors. We fell into a deep sleep around 3 AM.

I heard Chuck say, "It is better to check sooner rather than later." I bolted from my bunk and checked the screen. On the radar a large container ship was bearing down on us about one nautical mile away. Grabbing the VHF radio, I called the ship to make sure its captain saw us, fearful we were on a collision course. We were hove to, not able to respond quickly. He answered, stating that he saw us. We would be fine.

"I'm so glad that you told me to check our position," I said to Chuck as we breathed a sigh of relief.

He shook his head, "I didn't. I was sound asleep until you woke me up calling the ship to give our position."

Who knows if we were in any real danger that night? It was clear to me that something happened to ensure that we did not collide with the ship that was bearing down on us.

George Pratt

My dad was a very caring, but uneducated man. He did not finish high school. After attending a business school, he began working as a bookkeeper. I am the middle child and was the first to attend college. Dad was proud of my academic achievements and very supportive. He, perhaps more than anyone, looked forward to my college graduation in December 1965.

Early on Friday afternoon, thirteen days before graduation, I got a foreboding feeling that I needed to go home. I had not been home for several months. Twenty-four hours later, at age 53, Dad had a massive heart attack and fell in the hallway of our house. I was there to hold him.

He was unable to speak. "Dad, squeeze my hand if you hear me," I said. He squeezed. "The paramedics have been called. Hold on." He squeezed my hand again. "Do you hurt badly?" Without responding he breathed his last breath. I always wondered if he hurt or simply did not hear me.

Later on, not only did I become a tenured college professor in psychology, but a seasoned sailor, often single-handling my boat on the Chesapeake Bay.

In the summer of 1980, I made a trip to Bermuda on a 32-foot ketch with two other people. We expected the trip to take five to seven days. Leaving Norfolk we knew there was a small tropical depression we would have to pass through, but all of us had sailed in bad weather. We weren't worried. Besides, the trip to Bermuda is often complicated by squalls. What we did not know was that the tropical depression would turn into a tropical storm and stall in our path. We gravely misjudged the severity of the weather. By the beginning of the second day we had burned out the motor, and by the third day we had winds of 50 knots and had been struck by lightning, losing our radio and navigation equipment. Unable to take sun sights because of the torrential downpour, we had no idea where we were. The boat could not be kept dry. We always had one person in the cockpit, one manning the pump, and one tied to a bunk trying to rest. This continued for five days.

I always took the midnight-to-dawn watch so I could not see the massive waves that threatened us. The fetch, the distance between crests, was probably a mile. In the bottom of the wave you could hear and talk normally. At the top, where the wind blows, the noise was deafening. Add to that, the spray from the tops of the waves stung like wind-blown sand.

On the fifth night of the storm, I was in my bunk, trying to rest before I went back out on watch. The boat was being thrown around so violently we had not slept in several days. Suddenly, I heard music. "Do you hear music?" I asked the other person in the cabin. "No." I lay there and listened to Dan Fogelberg singing "Leader of the Band." I always assumed it was a song about his father. When the song ended, I heard my dad's voice.

"George, I know how scared you are right now . . . but don't be. This is not your time. The storm will clear by sunup. And, I want you to know that I did not hurt."

I relaxed and went to sleep. When the owner of the boat came in to wake me up for my watch he said, "I'm sorry, George, but we're heading into another thunderstorm."

I told him quite confidently, "It's OK. The storm will clear by morning."

He sighed and shook his head, "I don't think so. It doesn't appear to be clearing at all."

That night the waves were just as bad as ever, but I wasn't afraid. Next morning, exactly at dawn, the sun broke through the clouds. By 9:00 AM the weather had completely cleared. We took a sun sighting and headed for Bermuda.

When this happened, the psychologist in me wanted to call

> it a stress reaction, or lack of sleep, but I knew better. A stress reaction could not explain the specific prediction: "The storm will clear by sunup."

It is not only familiar voices that speak to us—husband, father, or those who have passed on. A voice can be the direct voice of Spirit, which speaks to all of us at every turn, on land or sea, showing us we are not alone. In the next story, you will read about a woman lost in the desert and hear how Spirit not only gave her the instructions for her current situation, but as it turned out, for her life.

Kate Eastman

> We were herding horses across 250 miles in Wyoming. At one point, wild mustangs chased our mares and we ran for a long time trying to get the mares back. Near the end of the day we got lost. The previous day when I saw my first eagle, I knew it was a sign of something to come. The group was divided in terms of which direction we should go. Half stayed behind. Half of us headed across a span of desert that someone believed to be the right direction. We were trying to make it across before the sun went down.
>
> My horse was the last to water, so I was at the end of the group. Because we were trying to beat the sun, we were running at a very fast pace. My horse began to slow down. I yelled to the rest of the group but they couldn't hear me because they were riding so fast. Then my horse really slowed down. At first I could see the group, and then I couldn't. Very quickly it became clear, I was alone, in the desert in the dark. I had no sense of which direction to go in. First, I cried. Then, I prayed. As I sat alone in the dark, a voice I call my Wise Woman said, "Let go of the reins." Now I had trained really hard for this trip, including how to ride without reins, so I literally let go of the reins. The horse immediately turned and started to run in a 180-degree direction

> from where we were. She ran exceptionally fast, scaring me as she jumped over holes and sagebrush in the dark. I trusted that she would not only lead me in the right direction, but not throw me off, leave me alone, injured, in the desert. Twenty minutes later in these conditions, we met up with the group.

The voice of Spirit answered Kate. It made a clear statement, with no judgments, shoulds, or possible terrible endings. It simply said, "Let go of the reins." Maybe it took an extreme situation for her to ask for help or to actually listen. We will probably never know if the circumstances made her better equipped to hear in the desert.

It is my opinion that we are innately tethered to this readily available unseen world of Spirit. We are born knowing this is a magical, mysterious Universe. We arrive with the ability to communicate mind to mind, to understand the language of rivers and trees, to heal ourselves and injured animals, to hear whispers of angels, to dream our world into being, and to see our destinies written in the stars. We are born knowing that wisdom resides in the souls and spirits of human beings and is revealed in who we are, not in what we say.

Somewhere along the journey we call life, we forgot these things. In our rush to grow up, life's mysteries were edited and re-edited right out of our souls. We developed a fixed idea about how the world works, and our original wisdom got lost in a new, more limited knowing. That's the trouble with knowledge—the more we think about something, dissecting and analyzing, the less we understand it. We have been trained to pursue knowledge, which is information borrowed from someone else. It is something to be possessed.

The only way to remember our original wisdom is to realize that we have adopted a narrow way of thinking about the world. We need to ask, "Who am I? Why am I here? What is the meaning of life?" A hidden order presents us with a meaning for life, but we have to find it and experience it for ourselves.

Not everyone forgets who they are and where they came from. I suspect that the closer we are to our birth, the more we remember. A nine-year-old boy named Austin Bell remembered. Perhaps his purpose for being here was to help us remember, to help us step beyond who we think we are and, for a moment, turn our attention from the world. We need these memories if we are ever going to break free of our limiting beliefs.

Austin Bell

Austin left his physical body in 2002. This story is told by his mother, Kimberly Bell.

> Austin saw angels everywhere. He described them as flecks of light, like motes of dust turning in a shaft of light, except they were bigger and brighter. At the time I could not see angels, but I could sense them. Since his death I also see them. One day I went into his room and said, "I think I have three angels around me. It's like I smell their perfume."
>
> Austin looked at me and smiled, "Oh, you have way more than three angels, Mom." Surprised at his response, I thought for a moment then asked,
>
> "What are angels?"
>
> "We are all angels. Here, while we are on Earth and in Heaven. It's all the same . . . And we are here to love, that's our purpose."
>
> "Austin, how do you know this information?"
>
> "You knew this too, Mom. You just forgot when you grew up."

Confucius said that the journey of a thousand miles begins with a single step. Remember that finding a hidden order starts with one small step. That step is a willingness to be open to the possibility that the most profound truths about our world and our destiny and the power to direct our lives into a future that we participate in creating, lie within reach. Our purpose is no less than a search for God. Our journey no less than a return to Spirit. What are we waiting for?

Experiential Practice

In the Introduction I asked you to consider the possibility that a hidden order is rapidly making itself known, that a spiritual evolution is taking place. I see this evolution as a paradigm shift in consciousness where we would view the world more holistically, as an integrated whole rather than a dissociated collection of parts. We would experience a sense of belonging, of connectedness to the cosmos as whole. We would be deeply, ecologically aware. The following exercises are to help you understand your connection to nature and to a hidden order.

Getting Started

The dimension of dreams is the same dimension that we vision when we journey to the Temple of Understanding. Our dreams are the link between Spirit and our waking consciousness, between Spirit and nature. Revisit the Master Practice exercise, Dreams, in chapter 11. Then continue on with the exercises below.

Daybook

Describe an event or situation in your life. Now back away emotionally, become the observer and describe it again, using a metaphor from nature. You might think of the situation as a tree. What kind of tree is it? Where is it growing? What does it need for nourishment? What are in its branches? Or choose another metaphor. Perhaps the situation can be described more easily as a body of water—an ocean, lake, or river. What does the color, temperature, and movement of the water tell you about the event?

Imagine that you are the tree or the water. Journal how you feel.

By aligning your life with the language of nature and the rhythm of a hidden order, you will begin to better understand its purpose and significance.

Tool Bag

Find an animal that you can spend time with. It can be a pet, a bird, an animal in nature. Quiet your mind and start following your breath. Then simply observe the animal. Do not attempt to interfere with what it is doing. Just observe.

Food for Thought

> For more than 99 percent of human history, the world was enchanted and man saw himself as an integral part of it. The complete reversal of this perception in a mere four hundred years or so has destroyed the continuity of the human experience and the integrity of the human psyche. It has very nearly wrecked the planet as well. The only hope, or so it seems to me, lies in the re-enchantment of the world.
>
> —Morris Berman, science historian

Invocation

Repeat the following to yourself:

> I walk the path of a hidden order, of the divine pattern that underlies all existence. I affirm my relationship with all others and with nature. May any obstacles that hinder peace and good relations become apparent so that, with the help of the Great Spirit, they will be transformed for the highest good of all. May my role on this earth be made clear.

Ritual

The following ritual is Tsalagi (Cherokee). The Temple of Understanding is the collective or cosmic consciousness, similar to the Akashic Records. The concept of the Akashic Records, or Book of

Life, can be traced back to the Semitic peoples, including the Arabs, the Assyrians, the Phoenicians, the Babylonians, and the Hebrews. Each of these peoples believed that the history of humankind—every word, deed, feeling, thought, and intent of every individual who has ever lived on Earth—was recorded on some kind of celestial tablets.

Within the Temple of Understanding, which is within and around us, is a great library where the records of all things are kept. This library contains information about your present life, past lives, and future lives, all of which are taking place simultaneously.

This ritual will work best if it is read aloud to you so that you can relax and simply follow along. So you might want to have someone else lead you in the journey, or record it in your own voice. If you do decide to record it yourself, make sure that you leave enough space and time between the directions so that you do not feel rushed. The ellipses (. . .) mean for you to pause. The word "pause" appears in parentheses when you might want even more time to reflect.

Like all vision quests, this one requires preparation. You will need to read the directions thoroughly before beginning. First, review the basics of how to relax in chapter 10. Next, set an intention that you wish to visit the Temple of Understanding in order to gain a deeper understanding of your place in a hidden order and of those things that stand in the way of reaching your highest potential.

Select a quiet, comfortable place for the journey where you will not be disturbed. Because our body temperature frequently changes during relaxation, you might wish to cover yourself with a light blanket. I suggest that you play a drumbeat such as David and Steve Gordon's *Sacred Earth Drums* in the background.[5] The music will act as a catalyst to reinforce the ritual and carry you deeper into your inner space. However, if you are someone who finds music distracting, then you will be better off without it. Keep your daybook close by, so that you can record your experience when you return.

When you are ready, start the music, loosen any tight clothing, and make yourself comfortable. As you listen to the beat of the drum, bring your awareness to your breath. Inhale as fully as you can, down into the core of your body. With each inhale and exhale you relax more and more. Do this a few times.

Now imagine that there is a white light that flows from the Universe down through the top of your head and slowly down through your body. The light moves down the back of your neck, your shoulders, your back, down your arms to the palms of your hands and out the tips of your fingers. It moves through the core of your body to your legs and to the soles of your feet. If any part of your body is tense or has pain, breathe in and bring the warmth of the white light into the tension, releasing it as you exhale. If any distracting thoughts occur, simply return your attention to your breath.

Now picture yourself on a trail that leads to the Temple of Understanding. Don't rush. Allow the image to become real to you.

Look around. What do you see? . . . (pause)

Look left . . . (pause)

Look right . . . (pause)

Look up . . . (pause)

Look down at the ground . . . (pause)

Look at the scenery . . . (pause)

What do you hear? . . . (pause)

What do you smell? . . . (pause)

Is there a breeze? . . .

Is it going to rain or is it hot and sunny, with no clouds in the sky?

As you relax and feel at peace and truly grateful that you are here, you begin to feel different—perhaps your body is tingling all over or maybe it's simply growing warmer. You feel the excitement in the air and you sense that you are close to the Temple.

In front of you, a translucent, twinkling light appears. As you watch it begins to shift into a shape . . . it is the Temple of Understanding.

Someone stands at the door and beckons you to come in . . . (pause)

You step inside . . . you see the fire that cannot burn and does not smoke. You see that you are surrounded by volumes of books that seem to go on forever. Take a moment to look around. Perhaps it is a library like none you have ever seen . . . (pause)

Affirm your purpose for being here . . . (pause)

Ask for help in reviewing your life . . . a book may automatically open up before you or you may choose to take one off the shelf. Or help may come to you in a different form altogether. Pay attention to everything you hear, see, smell, taste, and feel . . . (pause)

Once you feel you have received all of the information available to you for this journey, compare what you have learned to what you've done in your life so far. Is your pattern and style of living in harmony with your purpose for this lifetime? . . . (pause)

If not, throw anything that does not align with a hidden order and your mission into the fire . . . (pause)

Release to the fire anything that no longer serves you or stands in the way of you achieving your fullest potential . . . Take as long as you need and understand that anything that happens here does not have to make sense to you in this moment. Nor do you have to get all of the information you desire during this visit . . .

(I suggest that you pause for 3–5 minutes here.)

Knowing that you can come back to the Temple again and again, you leave and return to the trail . . .

As you come down the trail, return your awareness to your breath . . . (pause)

When you are ready, stretch your fingers and wiggle your toes and return to full waking consciousness.

In your daybook, write down everything you can remember about your vision quest. If you have difficulty in remembering parts of it, simply make it up for now. Everything comes from the same Source.

Part 2

Master Practices

9
Ego and Beliefs

> It is important that students bring a certain ragamuffin barefoot irreverence to their studies; they are not here to worship what is known, but to question it.
>
> —Jacob Chanowski

Ego

Carl Jung saw the ego as a kind of forceful unity, which binds, or fails to bind, the individuality. What Jung meant was that our ego is our conscious individualistic mind. He felt the ego was the center of consciousness—the sum total of our thoughts, ideas, feelings, memories, and perceptions. Many people and schools of thought use the term ego differently. For our purposes here, I am defining ego as everything we see about ourselves. It is that part of ourselves that identifies with our physical body and its senses, and appears to be separate from its surroundings. What is inside of the skin is me, what is outside of the skin is not me.

In esotericism, the ego is the Self. In *The Zelator*, Mark Hedsel describes the Self as ". . .a droplet of the Universal Mind, or Godhead."[1] Our problem is that until we realize that we are much more than our ego, we can become blinded by its perspective—believing it to be the only perspective. Our spiritual disciplines continually tell us to be mindful of our ego, for it separates us from the "All that is." Jung himself said:

> An inflated consciousness is always egocentric and conscious of nothing but its own existence. It is incapable of learning from the past, incapable of understanding contemporary events, and

> incapable of drawing right conclusions about the future. It is hypnotized by itself and therefore cannot be argued with. It inevitably dooms itself to calamities that must strike it dead.[2]

It is easy to get lost in trying to sort out the spiritual warnings of ego/no ego. The point to remember is that we can still enjoy life and be aware of our ego. We just need to understand its need to be in control. Just as a child cannot experience life in the world until it separates from its mother's womb, we cannot experience physical reality without separating from the womb of Spiritual Oneness. Each of us is a life force uniquely experiencing bungee-jumping, dancing, singing, writing; an energy that is an artist, a lover, a son.

To become adept at sensing a hidden order, we need to loosen our grip on "self," or ego, and allow the transpersonal perspective beyond this ego self to come forth. Our total beingness is dazzling beyond belief. By understanding our ego, we would be no less resplendent.

Ego Exercise 1

The Following the Breath—Quieting the Mind Practice in chapter 10 is meant to help us wake from being "asleep" or running on automatic. We are meant to pay attention in a particular way, on purpose, in the present moment, nonjudgmentally. Our intention is to sense an expanded version of ourselves. Quieting the mental chatter of the ego doesn't mean that our mind is necessarily silent, but rather that we move beyond the chatter. We allow thoughts to float across our mind like clouds floating across the sky; we don't hold on to them. We become aware that we are conscious creators of our lives, which unfold moment by moment; that we are part of and connected to everything; and that we are much more than our physical body.

This exercise is about awareness. After you begin your practice of following your breath, notice your thoughts and feelings about the practice itself. Do you feel the need to tell anyone that you are doing it or how wonderful it is? If you do, ask yourself why. It could be your ego talking.

Ego Exercise 2

If you are walking a spiritual path in search of going beyond the limits of ego, watch your thoughts. Notice when you magnify your status by name-dropping, boasting, judging, or mentally comparing yourself to someone else. Observe all of your thoughts.

Beliefs

How we choose to live our lives has everything to do with what we believe. Belief systems are the filters through which we perceive, assimilate, and internalize experiences, events, or things in order to give them meaning. Our view of how the world operates is a result of our beliefs.

For the most part, we have adopted our beliefs to protect our ego selves. Our beliefs serve to help us manage our environment. We can respond to our beliefs so quickly that they can appear to be instinctual—necessary for survival. We get so good at using our present beliefs—and many of them are useful—that we resist changing them.

Unfortunately, we frequently conclude that all of our beliefs keep us safe and we should do everything we can to fortify them. We gravitate toward others who hold the same, or similar beliefs; we habitually rely on the same beliefs and we seek out data that supports them, screening out anything that might weaken their stance. For example, my mother taught me that if I went outside in the winter with my hair wet I would catch a cold—and I did.

My belief about the nature of colds created tunnel vision, blocking from my view anything that did not support my position. With nothing to refute it, it became dogma: irrefutable truth, undeniable fact and insight on my part. For years I believed this self-fulfilling prophecy, totally ignoring the evidence—scientific journals and my observation of others—that suggested this was not an absolute truth.

Since I had no proof that I would not catch a cold, it took an act of faith for me to disregard my belief. My desire for change did not come from my head, but from my heart. Michael was a scuba diver. I wanted to be able to scuba dive with him in some seriously cold Maine water and weather. Knowing only that my belief about the way I caught colds was getting in the way, I had to try something different. Because the limiting belief came from my mother and I chose to believe her, it seemed reasonable that I could choose to believe something else. When you get rid of one belief you frequently replace it with another and, for the record, I have never gotten sick from having wet hair in cold weather since I took up scuba diving.

However, many of our cultural beliefs fall into the category of tunnel vision, and are not as innocuous. Our cultural gatekeepers including the media (newspapers and talking heads), authority figures (parents, teachers, doctors, ministers, priests, rabbis, politicians), and our friends and perceived enemies influence our beliefs by frequently supporting only the agreed-upon perspective. They can reinforce beliefs that our religion, whatever it may be, is the *only* religion.

Many believe that our way of life in the United States is a superior one. Some of our leaders believe that they know what is right for the masses and the rest of the world. If a different perspective is presented, it will not be heard. Instead, they will provide more imaginative reasons as to why the old, established view is the correct one. Those who challenge the old way or work to change the system often do so at great personal risk.

This is reinforced from an early age. We are taught to conform to the prevailing beliefs, rules, and preferred way of doing things. Once we decide to challenge convention and question these established beliefs that have been with us most of our lives not only is it risky, it takes great courage and willingness to be wrong. We do not know if we will meet with success and will find a better way. Yet when we hear a hidden order whispering, when we are frustrated with the status quo, when we hear our heart speak, do we have a choice? Where there is great risk, there is also tremendous potential. Scientific historian Thomas Kuhn, who uses the term paradigm in place of belief, puts our dilemma this way:

> The man [or woman] who embraces a new paradigm (belief) at an early stage must do so often in defiance of the evidence presented by problem solving. He must, that is, have faith that the new paradigm will succeed with the many large problems that confront it knowing only that the older paradigm has failed with a few. A decision of that kind can only be made on faith.[3]

Many of us sense a change taking place as consciousness evolves through us. Changes occur because the old way of being in the world no longer works. Einstein said it best when he observed, "No problem can be solved from the same consciousness that created it."

In *Discovering the Future,* Joel Barker talks about paradigm shifts. "I began to see why so many people in power had been so wrong over the last twenty years and why those same people were unable to identify and understand the major changes that were occurring. If the last twenty years have been marked by anything, they have been marked by the experts repeatedly missing important changes.[4] In "The New Business of Paradigms," his 2001 video, he goes on to say that we missed the World Trade Center because of a paradigm shift. And I believe much of the confusion we have about the future is because of the changes in paradigms."

To be comfortable with the fact of a new, evolving paradigm, we need to know what hidden beliefs we hold—what beliefs we have unconsciously embraced because of our science, religion, and society—so we can change them. To help you find these beliefs, I would like for you to read the following creeds created by transpersonal psychologist Charles Tart.[5] These creeds are "belief experiments" intended to illustrate how we have embraced science as fact and created our world, and ourselves, accordingly.

Read the creeds separately and slowly. Try to believe what you are reading. Dr. Tart recommends that you read them in a group, if possible, to illustrate how shared social activity influences our beliefs.

The Western Creed

I believe in the material universe as the only and ultimate reality, a universe controlled by fixed physical laws and blind chance.

I affirm that the universe has no creator, no objective purpose, and no objective meaning or destiny.

I maintain that all ideas about God or gods, enlightened beings, prophets, and saviors, or other nonphysical beings or forces are superstitions and delusions. Life and consciousness are totally identical to physical processes and arose from chance interactions of blind physical forces. Like the rest of life, my life and my consciousness have no objective purpose, meaning, or destiny.

I believe that all judgments, values, and moralities, whether my own or others', are subjective, arising solely from biological determinants, personal history, and chance.

Free will is an illusion. Therefore the most rational values I can personally live by must be based on the knowledge that for me what pleases me is Good, what pains me is Bad. Those who please me or help me avoid pain are my friends; those who pain me or keep me from pleasure are my enemies. Rationality requires that friends and enemies be used in ways that maximize my pleasure and minimize my pain.

I affirm that churches have no real use other than social support; that there are no objective sins to commit or be forgiven for; that there is no retribution for sin or reward for virtue other than that which I can arrange, directly or through others. Virtue for me is getting what I want without being caught and punished by others.

I maintain that the death of the body is the death of the mind. There is no afterlife and all hope of such is nonsense.

Close your eyes, notice your breath. Put your hand on your heart, how do you feel? Ask yourself what parts of this creed are true descriptions of reality? What do you personally know to be true?

Have you tested these beliefs or have you simply accepted them on some other authority as true? How many of these beliefs did you consciously choose? Journal your thoughts and feelings.

This book takes a different approach to the direction set by the above beliefs. It suggests that there is an underlying, organizing pattern to the Universe, that nothing is random, and that everyone has a unique contribution to life. This next creed, A Transpersonal Creed, affirms basic spiritual values. If either creed makes you think about what really matters, it has served its purpose. A Transpersonal Creed should be read experientially, like The Western Creed.

A Transpersonal Creed

I believe that the universe is spiritual as well as material, and that what happens to us is controlled by a combination of both physical and spiritual laws.

I affirm that human beings are part of an integrated Order of life; that we have considerable potential to evolve toward higher levels of this Order; and that seeking to evolve toward this Order is one of the highest values of human life.

I maintain that there are higher spiritual beings and enlightened humans. Life and consciousness seek to evolve toward these higher, nonphysical manifestations, even though currently rooted in the physical. Like the rest of life, my life and my consciousness share this purpose and destiny.

I believe that while some judgments, values, and moralities are subjective and personal, some are based on a valid intuition of higher possibilities. Those who help me understand and develop these higher possibilities are my friends and teachers; those who hinder me should be helped as much as possible. Insofar as all Life may be one Being, in a real and transpersonal sense, we should seek to maximize our love of and minimize our harm to all Life.

> I affirm that churches or other transpersonally oriented activities may sometimes be useful for aiding my and others' spiritual evolution; that there are actions that are objectively wrong, which we should avoid committing once we understand their nature; that there is a real and objective sense in which harming others harms myself and life; that the Universe is lawful on mental and transpersonal levels as well as physical levels, so all acts have consequences that must eventually be faced. Virtue for me is loving and helping myself and others, so Life and I may evolve.
>
> I maintain that the death of the body may not be the death of the mind. While hope of an afterlife can be rationalization for lack of evolutionary effort in this life, the probable reality of transpersonal levels of existence not dependent on a physical body may mean that individual life is much greater than physical life.

Close your eyes, notice your breath. Put your hand on your heart, how do you feel? Do you feel differently after reading this creed? What parts of this creed are true descriptions of reality? What do you personally know to be true? Have you tested these beliefs or have you simply accepted them on some other authority as true? How many of these beliefs did you consciously choose? Journal your thoughts and feelings.

The Buddha told his disciples, "Do not believe anything simply because you have heard it." And so you must question. Question your beliefs. Question what you think you know. Question.

10
Following the Breath—Quieting the Mind

> When you really look for me, you will see me instantly—you will find me in the tiniest house of time.
>
> —Kabir

Being able to relax and quiet your mind is essential to connecting with greater aspects of yourself and *A Hidden Order.* The heart of Buddhist meditation, quieting the mind is about becoming aware, waking up from the automatic pilot state that we run on. Most of us live in a robotic sleep state in which we miss the present moment, which is really all that we have. We lose touch with who and what we truly are. We don't take time to listen to those we love. We overlook synchronistic events and ignore intuitive whisperings, because the only voice, or thought that we hear, is the one that is loudest.

By cultivating the ability to follow your breath and quiet your mind you will become aware that you are an intricate part of the web of life. Following the breath isn't hard to do. You will find that after doing this exercise a few times you will be able to think "relax, center," and you will be there (or here in the present moment).

We use the breath to focus our attention because it is always present—always here in the existing moment. Paying attention to our breath as we inhale and exhale gives us an anchor to return to when our mind begins to sail out to sea, leaving the present moment for past memory or some distant, anticipated future. When the mind becomes distracted, breath by breath we can gently return to the present.

One of the key features of this or any other exercise is preparation. Drink enough water before practice so you will not be thirsty and go to the restroom if necessary before starting. If you are wearing glasses, remove them. Loosen all tight clothing, belts, watches, and shoes. Turn off the telephone. Set aside all concerns and worries.

Sit comfortably in a chair with your feet flat on the floor, or if you like, you may lie down on your bed or the floor. Loosen any clothing that is tight. Close your eyes.

To begin, simply notice your breath. Do not think about breathing deeply or trying to control how you are breathing. Just observe your breath. If your mind wanders, return your focus to your breath.

After practicing the above technique, alternate it with the following:

- Lie down, close your eyes, and begin to relax your body one part at a time. Starting at the top, hold your attention on your head as you inhale and allow your crown, ears, and face to relax as you exhale. Do the same for your neck, shoulders, chest, and so on until your entire body is relaxed.
- Slowly inhale through your nose and imagine that your breath is being drawn down into your lower abdomen. Your lower abdomen should expand naturally when you do this.
- Relax your tongue and allow your mouth to open slightly. Exhale slowly. You can exhale through your nose and your mouth simultaneously. Your lower abdomen should deflate naturally.
- After exhaling completely, let your breathing pause briefly in a natural way. Leave your tongue relaxed and your mouth slightly open. Your abdomen should also remain slightly collapsed.
- Continue to slowly inhale through your nose, exhale through your nose and mouth, and pause momentarily before inhaling

through your nose again. Keep your mind open and free during each full breath. Return your attention to the breath when your mind wanders.

Once you become accustomed to this method of breathing, begin practicing it while saying to yourself, "I am calm and relaxed." You might use the universal sound of "Om." Silently repeat Om to yourself in time with your breathing and the movement of your mouth and tongue. This technique flows as follows:

- Close your mouth lightly, rest the tip of your tongue on the roof of your mouth behind the front teeth, and slowly inhale through your nose. While breathing in, feel your breath being drawn down into your lower abdomen and think to yourself, "I am."
- Let your tongue relax and your mouth open slightly. Exhale slowly through your mouth and allow your abdomen to collapse naturally as you think the word "calm."
- After exhaling completely, let your breathing pause naturally and keep your mouth and tongue as well as your lower abdomen relaxed and in the same position. Think the words "and relaxed" while your breathing is paused momentarily.

Continue breathing and repeating your affirmation in this way for the duration of your practice period. When you are finished, do not stand up too quickly or immediately return to your everyday tasks. Instead, gently return your focus to your surroundings and do the following:

- Slowly open your eyes and gently rub your face with your hands.
- Massage the back of your neck using both hands.
- Stand up slowly.

- Shift your weight from leg to leg while briskly moving your arms and legs back and forth in a shaking motion.
- Stand up on your toes and drop back down onto your heels. Repeat this movement several times.

11
Dreams

Dreams are real, while they last. Can we say more of Life?

—Havelock Ellis

The Aboriginal people of Australia believe that dreamtime is the "time before time," or the "time of the creation of all things." According to their legends, all life is part of an unlimited network of relationships that can be traced to the Great Spirit Ancestors of the Dreamtime. The Ancestors created and govern the seasons, the growth of natural vegetation, reproduction, and the cycles of life from birth to death. They taught the Aboriginal people how to live in harmony with nature and with each other. Much of what the dreamtime stories suggest—the origins of man in Australia, and the Australian landscape as it is today—can be substantiated by scientific investigation.[1]

To the Aboriginals, every meaningful activity, event, or life process that occurs at a particular place leaves behind a vibrational residue in the earth, just as plants leave their image in seeds. The shape of the land, mountains, rocks, riverbeds, and waterholes and their unseen vibrations reflect the events that brought that place into creation. Everything in the natural world is a symbolic footprint of the metaphysical being whose actions created our world. The potency of an earthly location is wedded to the memory of its origin. This energy and sacredness of the earth, they call dreaming because only in expanded states of consciousness can one be aware of, or attuned to, the inner dreaming of the earth.[2]

Aboriginal art, created from this expanded state of consciousness, appears to be very abstract until you look at it from the point of view of being above the landscape. Then the picture shifts into focus—campfires, snakes, marks in the sand where men and women sit—everything becomes apparent. We can only suppose that when they create, Aboriginal artists *fly* above their landscape.

Regardless of what we believe about the dreamtime, the information that the Ancestors passed on about how to be in harmony with all life, how to be responsible leaders in the community, and what it means to be well versed in sacred law—may account for the fact that the Aboriginals have the longest continuous cultural history of any group of people on Earth, dating back by some estimates 65,000 years.

In a similar manner, dreams have had a profound effect on our history, but historians rarely mention the prophecies, discoveries, and achievements that came from the dream state. Throughout history, dreams have changed our world. For instance, most of the events surrounding the birth and early years of Christ were foretold in dreams; the Buddha's mother learned she had immaculately conceived in a dream;[3] Muhammad received his sacred calling in a dream, and much of the Koran was revealed to him in his dreams; Samuel Taylor Coleridge awoke from a dream with the poem, *Kubla Kahn;* Robert Louis Stevenson dreamed the plot of *Doctor Jekyll and Mister Hyde;* Mendeleev awoke with virtually the entire image of the periodic table of elements; Kekulé dreamed of dancing snakes biting their own tails, leading him to the cornerstone of modern chemistry (benzene molecules are closed circles); and Carl Jung decided to write *Man and His Symbols* for the general public after waking from a dream.

More recently, the late Joseph Shabalala, founder of the singing group Ladysmith Black Mambazo, was quoted as saying that every time he sleeps he has music on his mind. "There is a stage, but there are not children on the stage. They are between the stage and the sky, floating and always singing. They are like my teachers who teach me exactly this sound."[4]

Edgar Cayce believed that dreams were tools for transformation, offering us a window into our future. "We dream in advance of anything of importance that will happen to us."[5] Abraham Lincoln would probably agree. Just days before his death, President Lincoln dreamed that he awakened in the night and heard subdued sobs. He wandered from room to room throughout the White House until he reached the East Room where he came upon a throng of civilians and military guards surrounding a corpse. "Who died?" he asked. "The President. He was killed by an assassin."

Psychiatrist Ian Stevenson interviewed numerous individuals who dreamed the fate of the Titanic and canceled their trip. One English businessman, J. Connon Middleton, dreamed the same dream for two successive nights ten days before she sailed, ". . . I saw her, [the Titanic,] floating on the sea, keel upwards and her passengers and crew swimming around her." In the dreams he seemed to be floating in the air, just above the wreck.[6]

A friend of mine dreamed that two huge birds flew into two tall buildings, causing them to collapse, several months prior to September 11, 2001.

If many of our world religions, scientific discoveries, artistic endeavors, inventions, and innovations originated in the dream state, why would we choose to ignore our dreams, casting them off as meaningless and a waste of time?

Because, for the most part, our culture believes that the process of rational thought is the only legitimate source of knowledge—of Truth. In his landmark book, *Our Dreaming Mind,* Robert Van de Castle speaks to this belief when he says, ". . .we have become an unbalanced society, in which technology is viewed as the ultimate achievement. Our fascination with machines that can clear hundreds of acres of rainforest in a single day, machines that can unleash instant destruction on those with whom we politically disagree, and machines that, in speeding communication, tend to homogenize our opinions into a common ideological cast—threatens our continued existence on this planet."[7]

Could dreams be fundamental to understanding all existence? Suppose that everything in our material world and beyond originates with a thought. Consider that we sleep, not simply to rest, but to merge with our spiritual nature, to become part of a hidden order. In the dream state, our habitual way of thinking is suspended. Not bound by conventional beliefs—rigid rules of how to think—ingenious leaps that create and change the future are possible. In essence, we dream our world into being.

Our connection to the magical realm of dreams is what I call the dreamteller. Like the Aboriginals, capable of expanding their awareness into other realms day or night, our dreamteller is available to us anytime we need additional insight or wisdom.

During our waking hours when we hit a wall or a roadblock with something we are working on, and no matter how hard we try, the solution does not come, our dreamteller will whisper to us. We need to take a break, withdraw from the task at hand, let go, and let our ideas mingle around, just below the threshold of consciousness. Eventually our musings will merge, giving us the knowledge that we seek. For years I used running as a meditation, a way to clear my mind, hear my dreamteller, and bring information forward. Almost as soon as my feet would hit the pavement, solutions and answers would flow into my mind, so much so that I began to carry a tape recorder with me, to catch the thoughts.

Running may have brought answers to my immediate questions, but my dreams changed my beliefs about reality. After I made my decision to dissolve my sixteen-year marriage, I kept second-guessing myself—wondering if I had made a mistake. Frequently I fell asleep, asking my dreamteller for guidance.

Because my dachshunds woke at five AM, I got into the habit of letting them out, feeding them, and then going back to bed. Those early morning hours I would dream the answers to my conscious and subconscious questions that I carried on my heart.

One of these mornings, I had the last dream of a series. I was riding in a car with my ex-husband when the road we were on dead-ended. We got out of the car and walked through a graveyard. I ended up in a house that was sinking into the mud. The backside of the house was totally open—it had no walls. When I walked out of the house I looked down and saw that I was carrying a bag of garbage in each hand. I put the bags down and continued on.

After this dream, my dreamteller began to prepare me for marriage—I dreamed of a love seat, I selected a gown, chose my bridesmaids, picked flowers. These dreams were prophetic and symbolic, but not literal—I did not wear a wedding gown or have bridesmaids when I married Michael.

When we wean ourselves from the idea that there is only one fixed reality—one that we can touch, taste, hear, smell, and see—we sense that there is some vast creative force guiding the way, as though a hidden plan were being followed.

Our inherent potential, and connection to this creative force, is embodied in our dreams, and freed when we remember and work with our dreams. The more attention you pay to your dreams, the more you will remember, and the clearer they will become. As communication skills between you and your dreamteller are refined, you will find you have a new, reliable, and trustworthy direct link to a hidden order.

Remembering Your Dreams

How do we remember dreams? Intend to remember them. Our number one trap for not remembering our dreams is that we tell ourselves, "I never remember my dreams," "I don't dream," or "What I dream isn't important." Everyone dreams, we just don't always remember. But we can remember them if we intend to.

Support your intention to remember your dreams by placing a pen and paper, or a tape recorder, by your bedside. Create a ritual that tells your dreamteller you are going to pay attention. Ask a question before falling asleep.

You are looking for clarity. Ask one question at a time, not five at once. You may need to break your question into two or three separate questions, to be asked on different nights. If we ask five questions, we get five answers, all rolled up into what seems to be a singular response. Then we don't know which answer goes with which question.

Remember that if we are asking a question, somewhere in us, often hidden from consciousness, we already know the answer.

Wake up slowly. Immediately write down whatever comes to mind. If you do not remember your dream, and you have stretched or moved, roll back into the position you were in when you woke up. If you still do not remember your dream, make it up. Write your stream of consciousness. It all comes from the same source.

I believe that dreams present information that is life-enhancing. They come to tell us what we do not consciously know, not what we are already consciously aware of.

"But my dreams are so bizarre," you may say. "They make no sense."

Our dreamteller sometimes brings information from an expanded state of consciousness that words cannot adequately describe, where things are not necessarily linear or logical. When we do try to understand our dreams, or give meaning to the experience, commonly used words and descriptions seem limiting. Still, dreamteller sorts through our memory files, combining emotions, settings, places, word play, and characters—words and experiences that we will recognize,[8] to recount our dream experiences. It helps us see where we were and what we were doing or to answer the question that is on our heart.

In working to understand your dreams better, you will need to see differently. Try relating to the dream subject or object as if it is a personality. There are several ways to do this. You can become one of your dream subjects and interact with the other parts of the dream. For example, if you have a tree in your dream, become the tree. Ask yourself, as a tree, how you feel. "I am a tree. I am strong, yet flexible, important to the air humans breathe and the balance on the planet." Then ask how you connect with your surroundings.

Another way to gain insight is to separate yourself from the object. In this case, dialogue with the tree. "Why are you in my dream?" A thought will immediately come into your awareness. Write the thought down as the response from the "tree."

And lastly, consider the tree as also being conscious. Maybe the tree chose the experience of being a tree. If it is in your dream, conceivably you have expanded your consciousness so that you can now sense that the tree also has a purpose—a reason for being in your dream.

Your daybook is an appropriate place to record your dreams. You may wish to create a section just for that purpose. Remember, the more you write down your dreams, the more you will remember them. When you review your dreams for clues that will help you answer your heart's question or provide the solution you are seeking, record the following in your daybook:

- The setting, time, and place.
- The plot or trigger points precipitating the action or a change in the scene. Are you unable to finish a task? Is someone always chasing you?
- Who is the cast of characters—friends or strangers?
- The feeling of the dream. When you finish your interpretation do

you feel uplifted, full of insight? If not, take another look. Dreams do not come to make us unhappy, rather they come to provide clarity.

- Notice any word play or homonyms. Words that are used, often with humor, provide another way of looking at a situation. A friend once told me he dreamed that he was in his woodshed, cleaning out the wood. He interpreted the dream to mean that he needed to shed his "woulds—I am always saying, 'I would do this, but . . .'" This is word play.
- When does the plot mature and reach its climax?

We have a tendency to want to reach a conclusion, but there are times when the best thing to do is to not attempt to interpret the dream, but simply be the observer in the experience. This leaves the door open for access to your greater source of energy and wisdom. You are united not only with yourself at a deeper level, but with everything in the Universe.

My feeling is that many, if not most, of our dreams are precognitive, giving us information about other dimensions of ourselves and/or the future. By recording your dreams you may begin to get a feeling for different types of dreams. There is more than one way of interacting in the dream state. And there is more than one way to understand what your dreamteller is telling you.

It is my belief that night dreams, daydreams, imagination, and imagery all touch the same source—a dimension beyond our present day reality. While many suggest that a daydream is fantasy, Einstein said his best work resulted from ideas that arose while engaging in something similar to daydreaming.

When we daydream, our ego lets go of control and creating is effortless. With practice we can access the creative source that lies just below our conscious awareness. If we continue to relax we move into the hypnogogic (twilight) state, which we usually only experience fleetingly upon waking or drifting off to sleep. Vivid imagery often flashes before our mind's eye and we receive information beyond our normal conscious awareness.

In addition to daydreams, there are two other types of dreams—usually occurring at night—which I will mention briefly.

- **Lucid dream:** A lucid dream is a dream in which you are aware that you are dreaming. Frequently a lucid dream will begin in the middle of a normal dream when you realize that you are performing some impossible or unlikely task, such as flying or meeting someone you know—either living or deceased. You may simply realize that everything you are experiencing is in a dream, or you may find that you are able to actually alter what you are doing.
- **Out-of-body dream:** The out-of-body dream is an experience in which a person seems to perceive the world from a location outside the physical body. I like the model of our body being contained within the soul, as opposed to the soul being in the body. When we have an out-of-body dream or experience we see things from a more expanded part of the soul. If I see myself sitting on the sofa, and I am physically standing in the kitchen, I have shifted my position of viewing from the location of my physical eyes.

Tools for Dreaming

Scientists studying sleep do not know why we sleep, except that it seems to be necessary for life. Dr. Eve Van Cauter and her University of Chicago sleep lab colleagues discovered that after as few as six days of restricting sleep to four hours per night, normal volunteers had an increased appetite for high carbohydrate foods—suggesting that without sufficient sleep our bodies move into an imbalanced, diabetic state. Also, experimental rats died when they were deprived of sleep for longer than two to four weeks. The cause of death was not clear.[9] Although we don't yet have all the answers, it appears that sleep is essential for maintaining health and well-being.

While most people need between seven and nine hours of sleep each night,[10] there are individuals who have a natural sleep cycle of four hours. They sleep, dream, wake up and write or read, then return to bed for another hour or so. It is important to know your optimal sleep requirements. Do not try and force yourself into a sleep cycle that is not normal for you. On the other hand, if you are shortchanging your sleep and dreamtime, you could be creating sleep disorders at night and fatigue during the day.

If you find yourself counting the hours till dawn, notice what you are telling yourself. Do you say, I must have eight hours of sleep or I will be unable to function tomorrow? Do you lie awake and worry? Are you stressed? Overtired? This is a good time to hand your problems over to your highest source of assistance: God, your angels, your dreamteller. Ask to have your concerns resolved.

Below are some suggestions for getting a good night's sleep.

Suggestions for a Good Night's Sleep

- Start by intending to get a good night's sleep.
- Create a bedtime ritual, such as taking a shower beforehand, reading something inspiring, or journaling about your day.
- Go to bed and get up at the same time every day.
- Exercise regularly, but not just before bedtime.
- Avoid napping during the day for longer than twenty minutes.
- Do not eat chocolate or drink caffeine four to six hours before bedtime and limit the amount of alcohol you drink after dinner. Alcohol can cause you to wake frequently.
- Take a warm bath infused with a calming fragrance like lavender, rose, or jasmine. Light a scented candle in the bathroom while you bathe.
- Listen to soothing music.
- Take vitamin B_6 just before bedtime. This will help you remember your dreams.

- Write your dream intentions in your journal.
- Sleep in a cool room. Your ideal sleep environment is cavelike: dark, quiet, and cool.

If you are a woman experiencing hot flashes and your dreams are taking a back seat due to insomnia, there are natural remedies (East and West) that may help. Herbalist Susan Weed suggests that you drink a cup of oatstraw infusion before bed, or sleep on an oat hull pillow to ease night sweats, anxiety, and headaches.[11] For options in traditional Chinese medicine, the American Association of Oriental Medicine maintains a referral base for licensed acupuncturists and herbalists (1-888-500-7999).

Bedtime Tea

A cup of bedtime tea may also help you attain a good night's rest. Here's a simple recipe.

1 tablespoon dried chamomile or one chamomile tea bag
One ½-inch slice of fresh ginger or ½ teaspoon dried ground ginger

Place the herbs and ginger in one cup boiling water and allow to steep for five to ten minutes. Add lemon and honey to taste.

Feng Shui

In the passive, receptive state during sleep, our bodies are less guarded and more susceptible to the surrounding feng shui of the room we are in. Feng shui expert Nancy SantoPietro writes that our bedroom, and in turn the bed, "have a profound effect not only on our health, but on the quality of our intimate relationships."[12] Her suggestions mirror feelings that I have held for a long time: Keep all work out of the bedroom. Remove your television. If you watch TV in the bedroom, usually the last thing you will hear before you go to sleep are sounds of murder and mayhem. Could it be that some of the disharmony in the world is fed by the fact television is influencing our collective dreams?

Televisions are also a high source of electromagnetic energy fields that can affect your health. Move them and any computers or clock radios at least six feet away from the circumference of your body, and never use an electric blanket.

Because beds and bedding carry different vibrations, the shape, color, and materials need to be selected with the impact most appropriate to you. For more detail, you may wish to consult one of the numerous books on feng shui.

Dream Pillow Ritual

My maternal grandmother had hand-stitched dream pillows on every bed. Each was filled with herbs and flowers to relieve headaches, alleviate sinus congestion, eliminate nightmares, and bring sweet dreams and/or needed information.

You will need:

- A square of dark blue cloth approximately 8 x 8 inches preferably made of natural-fiber cotton, silk, linen, or a blend of these
- Lavender or chamomile herbs
- Your choice of rose petal, mugwort, rosemary, or catnip

Form a bag by sewing two sides of the cloth together. Turn it inside out and fill it with herbs. Sew it closed or bring the corners together and tie them with a ribbon, string, or piece of yarn. Place the pillow close to your head, so that when you smell it in the night it will prompt you to recall your dreams.

Invocation

Earth, Air, Water, Fire
Dreamteller, hear my desire.
From veiled sleep to morning light
I will recall my dreams tonight.

12
Intention

Silent knowledge is nothing but direct contact with intent.

—Carlos Castaneda

When we discover our connection to a hidden order, the way we see life changes. We trust in a generous, eternal Universe, one that is always evolving and life-enhancing—one that is friendly and supportive. We become our authentic self and realize that we are the primary creative force in our life. In this state, we manifest for the good of the whole; to do harm is not in our consciousness.

It sounds wonderful. But perhaps the hardest thing in the world is to claim this power, to rid ourselves of doubt, to trust that we are a part of something greater. It is easier to take things personally. We feel angry or sad because we have no control in our lives. We are victim to external forces. Temporary satisfaction is had by blaming others. We feel justified in our complaints because someone else did something to us.

If we really believed that we are responsible for what happens to us on Earth, and for what we do on Earth after we leave it, we would do things differently. By not trusting in our greatness we create pain, suffering, and war because we have not learned to create anything else. To intend to align with a hidden blueprint and create balance is our next step—and is real power. By doing so, our path rises up to meet us.

Look inside of yourself. Notice how fast you are changing. This change is nonlinear, by which I mean that it takes place on multiple levels: your heart, your soul, your mind, your higher self, other lifetimes. Consciously choose to let go of the old, let things die when it is time for them to die. This can be relationships, beliefs, routines, even your career. Religious scholar Matthew Fox says that the real issue of letting things die is "the lack of faith—lack of trust—to allow things to be reborn. We don't trust the spirit, who touches and speaks to all people—who makes mystics of us all if we allow it to."[1]

If you are not creating consciously, you are creating unconsciously and you are remanifesting what you have created in the past. You will create the same painful relationships, the same sense of being victim, the same perception of being unworthy, until you wake up, in this lifetime or another, and say, "Ah. I see what I have been creating, I'm not going to do this anymore." You set your intention to create differently: to join with a hidden order, to be harmonious, cooperative, generous, and respect all life.

Intention is not a thought, a thing, an action, or an ambition, but an alignment with Spirit. It is our direct link to a hidden order. Intention makes us succeed when our thoughts tell us we have failed. It requires focus and awareness, mindfulness, and detachment.

Several years ago I was attempting to play golf with Michael. For the record, I am not a golfer. That day, I spent most of my time tilling the greens. After nine boring holes, I thought about my father, who did play golf. He used to tell me, "Golf is like the game of life. Every round is a journey, which ultimately leads you back to where you began, hopefully a little wiser. The ball is a symbol of perfection. It contains all potential because it is a sphere. When it is in flight it is a reminder to us that we can fly if we put our minds to it. If you can learn to focus your mind and send that little ball exactly where you want it to go, then you can focus your life and create it exactly as you would have it be. In this simple game is hidden the true secret of life."

Closing my eyes and setting my intention, I immediately visualized a very sharp, focused, and detailed moving picture of the golf ball rolling 25 feet over the green, toward the hole and dropping in.

It's hard to describe, but I was totally absorbed in that particular moment. There was a clarity that I can't explain. My perspective was at the ground level, looking directly at the golf ball in front of me. And there were only four things in the entire Universe—awareness, the golf ball, the putter, the hole. I opened my eyes, gripped the putter, and putted.

As if pulled by an unseen filament of destiny, the golf ball rolled exactly as I had imagined. It rolled 25 feet to the hole and dropped in.

In the grand scheme of things, whether or not I sank the golf ball is of little importance. But on my path of understanding, it was very important. I learned, through direct experience, how intent and imagery create our reality. No other thought came into my mind between my image of the path of the golf ball and my putt. For a brief moment in time, I stretched beyond my boundaries and touched the inconceivable . . . and an extraordinary event took place. Could I do it again? Not that day. I would visualize the shot, but stop to congratulate myself on my previous success. This attachment to my past accomplishment canceled out what I was trying to manifest in the present moment.

The underlying question is, how did this happen? It would seem that all of the elements of manifesting—what some would call real magic—were there. I had an extremely well-defined intent, yet I was not attached to the outcome. I wasn't playing for the Master's cup. I was simply attempting something that my father once suggested: "Focus your mind and send your golf ball exactly where you want it to go."

In that moment there were no conflicting desires that would cancel out my intent, which was simple—the golf ball drops into the hole. I focused my attention and visualized what I wanted to take place. Because my awareness was expanded, my intellect could not jump in and separate me from my intent, giving me all the reasons I would fail, or how great I would look by succeeding.

But there was still something else that took place on that green, in that moment when my state of mind was graced by extraordinary clarity. For the briefest of instants, I stepped into a magic realm that, I believe, has been here all along.

Gary Zukav was once asked if something happened to him between his writing of *The Dancing Wu Li Masters* and *The Seat of the Soul* that allowed him to write so profoundly about higher realities. He answered,

> Yes, I discovered nonphysical reality. I didn't know at the time that there was such a thing as nonphysical reality. But intentions of the soul operate at very deep places within us. You do your part by setting intentions consciously, to the best of your ability. That brings you into alignment with your soul, with your deepest sense of meaning.[2]

Intention

We are here to ask the question, why are we here? What is the meaning of life? What is a hidden order and how am I a part of it? Intention is our direct link to Spirit, to a hidden order. Remember, we are innately already connected.

Start with the step that is in front of you. There is no one way to discover a hidden order. We all take many different roads to reach the same destination. I have explored many spiritual paths: Episcopalian, Native American, Quaker, Buddhist, and Taoist. The following suggestions blend thoughts from various teachings. I offer them simply as a guide, not as "the way." The best advice I can offer is, stay open to change, refine your search as need be, and remember that a hidden order shows itself in many different forms. And last, but most important, do not insist upon discovering a final truth.

Look inward to discover who you are. When we turn inward, we see the world that we have created. If our heart is cold, so is our view of the world. When we are open to life, we are able to love unconditionally. If we are quiet, we hear the whispers that gently guide us.

Let things be. Try accepting things just as they are. You may wish it were sunnier, warmer, colder, or Friday instead of Monday. Simply be. Your mind will always create wants and try to change things. Let things be exactly as they are.

Observe energy (chi). Our Universe is flowing energy. This energy creates all of life. Spend time in nature watching the flow of a river, or the ocean. Feel the wind, watch a bird fly, or a child play.

Listen. Listen to the voice of your heart, your inner-mind, which is an extension of the mind of the Universe. Remain open to all forms of information. Do not judge the status of the messenger.

Be open to the subtle. If we get caught up in what we think is real we do not see a hidden order revealing itself. Our eyes focus on the material world. Learn to sense the world indirectly. Soften your gaze, look at a tree in your peripheral vision. Then turn and look slightly above the leaves on a tree or a plant. Look in-between the branches. Ponder your impressions. Open all of your senses. They connect us to the beauty, tastes, and smells of life and to invisible worlds.

Be attentive. Bring your awareness to the present moment, see everything as though you are a child, seeing it for the first time.

Be still. Several times a day, stop and stand still. Follow your breath. Absorb the quietness.

Do small things. Whatever you do, do it one step at a time. It is better to do small things in the present moment, where everything you need is available to you, than to do something grand absent-mindedly.

Create your own ideology. Do not rely on what you have been taught; rather, discover and cultivate your intuition. Then trust what you sense to be true.

Look for the opposites. Everything in life has its opposite, this is the creative pull. Beautiful/ugly, difficult/easy, rich/poor are all complementary parts of the whole. To understand the whole, look for the opposite and the complement of what you see.

Allow life to happen. Life is change, do not fear it. Stay open and attentive and do not try and hold on to that which wishes to change. Pursue only those things that are life-enhancing.

Do not attempt to grasp a hidden order. A hidden order can only reveal itself to you in the present moment. In its entirety it is inconceivable. Anything that we can fully comprehend and act upon is small and manageable. We see apparent contradictions only because the whole is too vast for us to conceive.

Leave yourself open to the opinions of others. Listen fully to what others have to say. There is always something that we do not know, an ever-evolving Universe of wisdom we have yet to experience.

Be comfortable not knowing. Be content to say, "I don't know."

Lead by being. Our attitudes affect others more than what we say or do. Shape events through the power of your attitude. Value qualities that everyone has—integrity, spontaneity, creativity, flexibility, not the possessions that they have acquired, or the social status they have reached. Remember that under the skin we are all the same.

Practice simplicity. Clear out and pare down. Create a sense of organization and order, internally and externally.

Let go of self-importance. You do not have to compete or push ahead of others to obtain your desires. Excessive force in any one direction triggers the growth of an opposing force. If your desires originate from your deepest source, a hidden order will bring them forth naturally.

Make space in your life for Spirit. Learn to say, "No." Leave your cell phone at home. Throw away your "shoulds." Sit and do nothing. Take a walk. You will find that everything still gets done, and you are more peaceful for having taken the time. Say "Yes" to spontaneity and play.

Move on. Nothing is stagnant in nature, everything grows, matures, and dies. When your work is done, move on, do not linger.

Resources

Books

For more scientific explanations of the information covered in *A Hidden Order,* I suggest the following:

Greene, Brian. *The Elegant Universe.* New York: W. W. Norton & Company, Inc.

McTaggart, Lynn. *The Field: The Quest for the Secret Force of the Universe.* New York: HarperCollins, 2001.

Talbot, Michael. *The Holographic Universe.* New York: HarperCollins, 1991.

Guided Imagery on CD available at **www.winterrobinson.com**

Winter Solstice
Woman's Lullaby
A Hidden Order

Sources of Tea

There are many excellent sources of tea. Three of my favorites are:

Kindred Spirit
1204 Simonton St.
Key West, FL 33040
(305) 296-1515
www.KindredSpiritKeyWest.com
Bookstore and tea room. They love their tea as much as their books!

Upton Tea
www.teatimeworldwide.com

Spicetopia
62 B Spanish St.
St. Augustine, FL 32084
(904) 808-8487
I highly recommend their tropical Rooibos from South Africa.

Yarrow Sticks

Jane English
PO Box 185
Calais, VT 05648
(802) 456-1004
www.eheart.com

Notes

Introduction

1. Thanks to Joanne McMahon, Ph.D., researcher in the nature of rituals, who provided me with the information on rituals.

Chapter 1

1. James Legge. *I Ching, the Sacred Books of China: the Book of Changes.* Dover Publications, 1975.
2. R. L. Wing, *The I Ching Workbook* (New York: Doubleday, 1979).
3. I am not alone in my belief that the *I Ching* is more than chance. Carl Jung was convinced that there was a deep and subtle wisdom underlying the *I Ching.* It was clear to him that for the *I Ching* to be able to maintain itself for over four thousand years, in a civilization as sophisticated as the Chinese, it must contain a secret that was well worth discovering.
4. Not his real name.
5. R. L. Wing, *The I Ching Workbook.*
6. Richard Wilhelm, trans. and C. F. Baynes, ed., *The I Ching or Book of Changes,* Bollingen Series XIX (Princeton, NJ: Princeton University Press, 1983).
7. Adeline Yen Mah, *Watching the Tree,* p.27.

Chapter 2

1. Malcolm Godwin, *The Holy Grail* (New York: Barnes and Noble, 1994.
2. Half the Upper Room is closed off. Behind a veil a long, wooden table is set for the "Last Supper of Christ." This powerful symbol reminds us of the awakening "Christ consciousness" that is the indwelling Spirit within us all.
3. Although this may sound preposterous to some, the recent work of Frenchman Michel Gauquelin supports the idea that there is a planetary effect on our personality. Gauquelin obtained 16,336 timed births of prominent professionals and 24, 961 of average professionals. He found that, for certain occupations, the presence at birth of a certain planet, that had either just risen over the horizon or reached its high point in the sky seemed to cause success—the Moon was significant for writers, Mars for sportsmen and soldiers, Saturn for doctors and scientists, and Jupiter for soldiers, actors, and writers. See his book *Cosmic Influences on Human Behavior* (Santa Fe, NM: Aurora Press, 1985).

4. B. Ghiselin, *The Creative Process* (New York: New American Library, 1980.)
5. Dirk subsequently died on this shallow reef, before the *Atocha* was discovered.
6. Al Siebert, Ph.D. may be contacted at PO Box 505, University Station, Portland, OR 97207.
7. Condensed from *Psychiatry Can Be Hazardous to Your Mental Health* by William Glasser, M.D., (New York: Harper Collins, 2003.)
8. The transformation experience can be a sudden awareness of a new truth you have never before dreamed of. You suddenly awaken to a new way of seeing, and being, in the world. Perhaps you realize you are connected to everything and everybody on the planet. Or, possibly you recognize your own habitual, destructive patterns and realize that you have to change immediately. Sometimes the transformation experience is the result of knowing things are changing—you suddenly know that your marriage is over, you are going to be fired from your job, or a new friend has just entered your life. The flash of insight may be momentary, but its effects will persist.
9. P. D. Ouspensky, *In Search of the Miraculous: Fragment of an Unknown Teaching* (New York: Harcourt, Brace, & World, 1949.)
10. Charles Tart, *Waking Up: Overcoming the Obstacles to Human Potential* (Boston: Shambhala, 1986.)
11. Jon Kabat-Zinn, *Wherever You Go, There You Are* (New York: Hyperion, 1994).
12. Roy Rowan, *The Intuitive Manager* (Boston: Little, Brown and Company, 1986.)
13. *Newsweek*, August 12, 2002. Note: In May 2003, according to a *Sunday Times* survey that estimates the fortunes of Britain's wealthiest people, author J. K. Rowling is richer than the queen. The *Times* estimates Rowling's fortune at $444 million.
14. *Readers Digest*, December 2000.
15. Charles Tart, *Living the Mindful Life* (Boston: Shambhala, 1994.)

Chapter 3

1. Plato, *The Republic,* Book X, translated by J. Wright.
2. Dhyani Ywahoo, *Voice of Our Ancestors* (Boston: Shambhala, 1987).
3. The Emerald Tablet of Hermes is the original source of Hermetic philosophy and alchemy. Although the language of the original version is in doubt, it is through the Latin version that the Emerald Tablet rose to preeminent fame as a key to the primary mysteries of nature: *As above, so below.*
4. Not his real name.
5. On October 19, 1987, the Dow Jones Industrial Average plunged 508.32 points, losing 22.6 percent of its total value.

6. Mickey Hart and Jay Stevens, *Drumming at the Edge of Magic* (San Francisco: HarperSanFrancisco, 1990.)
7. Joachim-Ernst Berendt, *Nada Brahma: The World Is Sound* (London: Inner Traditions Intl., Ltd., 1991.)

Chapter 4

1. Many esoteric teachings describe the human energy field, or aura, in great detail—some dividing it into several layers or bodies. Chi, or subtle energy, is essential to Chinese medical thinking. There is no English word that captures its meaning. Everything in the Universe is composed of and defined by its chi, but chi is not a primordial, immutable material. And it is not merely vital energy. Ted Kaptchuk, author of *The Web That Has No Weaver,* says, "We can perhaps think of chi as matter on the verge of becoming energy, or energy at the point of materializing."
2. Quakers believe in the power of the body to heal itself. They taught me the process of holding someone "in the light" for healing.
3. Larry Dossey, *Reinventing Medicine* (New York: HarperCollins, 1999).
4. Nancy SantoPietro, *Feng Shui and Health: The Anatomy of a Home* (New York: Three Rivers Press, 2002.)
5. Nancy SantoPietro, *Feng Shui and Health.* Thanks to my friend Nancy for suggesting these categories.
6. Diana Rosen, *The Book of Green Tea* (Pownal, VT: Storey Books, 1998.
7. Elizabeth Hightower, "Good Tea Hunting," *Organic Style,* (March-April, 2003), p. 93.

Chapter 5

1. Richard Wilhelm, trans. and C. F. Baynes, ed., *The I Ching or Book of Changes.*
2. Caroline Myss, *Sacred Contracts* (New York: Harmony Books, 2002.
3. Rob Brezsny, the astrologer/televisionary oracle, can be found at *www.freewillastrology.com.*
4. Sophie Burnham, *The Path of Prayer* (New York: Viking Press, 2002), p. 75.
5. Dennis William Hauck, *The Emerald Tablet* (New York: Arkana, 1999. The alchemists believed the Emerald Tablet was the basis for a spiritual technology first introduced on the planet before the Great Flood. That technology is based on a secret formula that consists of seven consecutive operations performed to perfect matter, whether it be of a physical, psychological, or spiritual nature. To hide the true meaning of their work, each step of the formula was described in chemical terms. Although the alchemists spoke of furnaces, flasks, and beakers, they were really talking about changes taking place in their own bodies, minds, and souls.

6. Robert Jahn and Brenda J. Dunn, *Margins of Reality* (New York: Harcourt, 1989.)
7. Susannah Seton, *365 Simple Pleasures* (Berkeley: Canari Press, 2001.)
8. John O'Donohue, *Anam Cara: A Book of Celtic Wisdom (*New York: Harper-Collins, 1997), p. 36.

Chapter 6

1. R. L. Wing, *The I Ching Workbook.*
2. Sea smoke is evaporation fog or steam fog, which is formed when water vapor is added to air that is much colder than the vapor's source, most commonly, when very cold air drifts across relatively warm water. Along coastal regions, such as the Gulf of Maine, sea smoke frequently arises in autumn and early winter when an arctic air mass slips off the continent onto the warmer Atlantic waters. Sea smoke can reduce visibility to near zero.
3. Mel Allen, "Don't Call Us Heroes," *Yankee Magazine*, February 1993. Also reported by Margot Brown McWilliams in "Sea Rescue: A Mix of Grit and Good Fortune," *Portland Press Herald*, January 21, 1992.
4. Carol Muske-Dukes, "In a Heartbeat," *O: The Oprah Magazine,* November 2001, 197-202. (See copyright page for permissions notice.)
5. Jim Shawvan, "The Red Planet," from *The Mountain Astrologer*, April 2001. I have taken the liberty of editing Jim Shawvan's article… to make it understandable in layman's terms.
6. Jeffrey Zaslow, "Robert's Rules of Order," *USA Weekend*, November 23–25, 2001.
7. David Maraniss, "September 11, 2001: Thousands' Workaday Scenario Turned Surreal," *Washington Post,* September 16, 2001.
8. David Maraniss, "September 11, 2001: Thousands' Workaday Scenario Turned Surreal."
9. Not her real name. These stories are true, but all names have been changed to protect the privacy of the individual.
10. Kahlil Gibran, *The Prophet* (New York: Alfred A. Knopf, Inc., 1923.)

Chapter 7

1. Diane K. Osbon, ed., *Reflections on the Art of Living: A Joseph Campbell Companion (*New York: HarperCollins, 1991.)
2. I use the feminine pronoun for God in this case because I believe that God is within each of us.
3. Maxwell Maltz, *Psycho-Cybernetics: A New Way to Get More Living Out of Life* (New York: Simon & Schuster, 1960).
4. R. L. Wing, *The Tao of Power* (New York: Dolphin-Doubleday, 1986.)

5. Richard Wilhelm, trans. and C. F. Baynes, ed., *The I Ching* or *Book of Changes.*
6. Doug Boyd, *Mad Bear: Spirit, Healing, and the Sacred in the Life of a Native American Medicine Man* (New York: Touchstone Books, 1994.)
7. Richard Wilhelm, trans. and C. F. Baynes, ed., *The I Ching* or *Book of Changes.*
8. *www.merkaba.org/sundays-scientific.php*
9. Orme-Davidson, et al. "International Peace Project in the Middle East: The Effect of the Maharishi Technology on the Unified Field," *Journal of Conflict Resolution*, vol. 32, 4 (1988): 776-812.
10. *http://noosphere.princeton.edu/terror.html*
11. R. L. Wing, *The Tao of Power.*
12. Peter Russell, *Global Brain* (Palo Alto, CA: Global Brain, Inc. 1995.)

Chapter 8

1. Phi is derived from the Fibonacci sequence (1, 1, 2, 3, 5, 8, 13, 21), famous not only because the sum of the bordering terms equals the next one (1+1=2; 2+3=5, and so on), but because the quotients of adjoining terms approximate the number 1.618—1/1 = 1, 2/1 = 2, 3/2 = 1.5, 5/3 = 1.666, 8/5 = 1.6, and so on.
2. Mario Livio, *The Golden Ratio: The Story of PHI, the World's Most Astonishing Number* (New York: Broadway Books, 2002).
3. Roger Nelson's work with the Global Conscious Project (see also chapter 7) lends credibility to this idea.
4. We can begin to sort out the types of voices we hear by what they say. For instance, we all have voices of our parents that we hear from time to time. These voices can be helpful, protective, or simply controlling and judgmental. It is up to you to discern whether to listen to the voice, or simply say, "Thank you for sharing, but I am going in this direction anyway."
5. Available from Sequoia, PO Box 3189, Ashland, Oregon 97520-3189. 1-800-524-5513.

Chapter 9

1. Mark Hedsel, *The Zelator* (York Beach, ME: Samuel Weiser, 2000.)
2. Carl Jung, *Psychology and Alchemy* in *Collected Works*, vol. 12, (Princeton, NJ: Princeton University Press, 1980), p. 563.
3. Thomas S. Kuhn, *The Structure of Scientific Revolutions* (Chicago: University of Chicago Press, 1962.)
4. Joel Barker, *Discovering the Future: The Business of Paradigms* (St. Paul, MN: ILI Press, 1989.)
5. Charles Tart, *Open Mind, Discriminating Mind* (San Francisco: Harper & Row, 1989.)

Chapter 11

1. Jennifer Isaacs, *Australian Dreaming: 40,000 Years of Aboriginal History* (Wolloughby, NSW: Ure Smith Press, 1988.)
2. *www.crystalinks.com/dreamtime.html*
3. Ania Teillard, *Spiritual Dimensions* (London: Routledge and Kegan Paul, 1961.
4. Robert Van de Castle, *Our Dreaming Mind* (New York: Ballantine Books, 1994). As seen in *Time Magazine*, August 10, 1987.
5. Suz Andresen, *Dreaming the Future: The Ultimate Dream Guide* (Virginia Beach, VA: ARE Press, 2001.)
6. Ian Stevenson, *A Review and Analysis of Paranormal Experiences Connected with the Sinking of the Titanic.* Reprinted from the *Journal of the American Society of Psychical Research*, vol. LIV, no. 4 (October 1960).
7. Robert Van de Castle, *Our Dreaming Mind.* As seen in *Time Magazine*, August 10, 1987.
8. Mary Watkins, in *Waking Dreams* (Dallas: Spring Publications, 1976), reminds us that the same source that creates our dreams—the imagination—is also responsible for limiting them because we not only have them describe themselves, we dictate the terms of the description we will perceive and value.
9. *www.sleepmedservices.com*
10. Robert Ballard, MD, director of the Sleep Disorders Center at the National Jewish Medical and Research Center in Denver in *Delicious Living*, March 2003, p. 72.
11. Susan S. Weed, *Menopausal Years, the Wise Woman's Way* (Woodstock, NY: Ash Tree Publishing, 1992.)
12. Nancy SantoPietro, *Feng Shui and Health.*

Chapter 12

1. Russell Decarlo, *Towards a New World View: Conversations at the Leading Edge* (Erie, PA: Epic Publishing, 1996), p. 68.
2. Russell Decarlo, *Towards a New World View*, p. 328.

About the Author

Winter Robinson is internationally recognized for her ability to incorporate and teach the intuitive process as a complement to medical diagnosis. At Brown University Medical School she designed and headed a pilot project for medical students that explored the limits of intuitive diagnosis. Her work has been featured in *Natural Health* magazine, *Mothering* magazine, *Utne Reader* and on numerous talk and radio shows.

Author of *Intuitions: Seeing with the Heart* and *Remembering: A Gentle Reminder of Who You Are,* she recently released three CDs: *Winter Solstice, Woman's Lullaby,* and *A Hidden Order*, a companion piece to this book.

Winter's work with her husband concentrates directly on helping individuals and organizations discover a more holistic method of using the mind—a method that taps into a client's frequently unused natural abilities and bridges the gap between ordinary problem-solving and creative innovation.

Winter lives outside Portland, Maine with her husband and their dachshunds, cats, chickens, and geese.

If you enjoyed *A Hidden Order* and would like to
know more about Winter's work or seminar schedule,
visit her at *www.winterrobinson.com.*

To Our Readers

Red Wheel, an imprint of Red Wheel/Weiser, publishes books on topics ranging from spunky self-help, spirituality, personal growth, and relationships to women's issues and social issues. Our mission is to publish quality books that will make a difference in people's lives—how we feel about ourselves and how we relate to one another and to the world at large. We value integrity, compassion, and receptivity, both in the books we publish and in the way we do business.

Our readers are our most important resource, and we value your input, suggestions, and ideas about what you would like to see published. Please feel free to contact us, to request our latest book catalog, or to be added to our mailing list.

Red Wheel/Weiser, LLC
P.O. Box 612
York Beach, ME 03910-0612
www.redwheelweiser.com